whimsical
woollies

Marie Mayhew

STACKPOLE
BOOKS

0 11557 00564 6

Published by
STACKPOLE BOOKS
5067 Ritter Road
Mechanicsburg, PA 17055
www.stackpolebooks.com

Printed in the United States of America

10 9 8 7 6 5 4 3 2 1

First edition

Cover design by Caroline Stover
Photography by Laurie Judd, John Mayhew, and Marie Mayhew

Library of Congress Cataloging-in-Publication Data

Mayhew, Marie.
  Whimsical woollies : 20 projects to knit and felt / Marie Mayhew. — First edition.
    pages cm
  ISBN 978-0-8117-0564-6
1. Felt work. 2. Felting. 3. Knitting. I. Title.
  TT849.5.M385 2015
  746'.0463—dc23
                                      2015004661

Contents

Acknowledgments

A special thank you to my parents, who encouraged creativity in their home, whether in writing, problem solving, or the arts. My dad is now in heaven, encouraging and watching out for me like he never could before.

With special love to my children, Isaac and Hannah, for their strength and belief in me and their living daily with the yarn mess and a house overflowing with little stuffed creatures—the results of all that writing, problem solving, and art.

In gratitude to my sister-in-law Laurie Judd for her creative eye and whimsical photography and making my patterns come alive.

I am grateful to the staff of Stackpole Books and especially to Pam Hoenig, my editor, for giving me this chance to have a bigger voice.

To my husband John, my dearest friend, my in-house designer, and the best encourager anyone could ever hope to have on their side, to you, I dedicate this book.

And finally, thank you to all the knitters over the years who have knit my patterns and then sent me such sweet notes and photos of their projects, encouraging me to keep on creating!

Introduction

I began playing with felting over fifteen years ago. My first felting experience was an ornament class, making miniature stockings and mittens to hang on my tree. Within two weeks I had made dozens in every yarn combination possible. I was in love! What I enjoyed most was the embellishing of these simple ornaments. Within a year I was asked to teach the same class. I thought the store was teasing me. What did I know about teaching felting? They assured me that my samples alone, enough to go around the block once, were their proof I could teach. I had become an authority and didn't even know it. And so my felting career began. Never would I have imagined where that one class would lead me.

I started out selling my patterns locally to yarn stores in my hometown, St. Paul, Minnesota. I began selling nationally after an ad was placed in *Vogue Knitting*'s annual felting magazine. I now have thirty patterns and a few kits to my name. Now years later, thousands of knitters around the world have knit my felting patterns. The Woolly Snowman pattern, included in this book, just recently celebrated the tenth anniversary of its first release.

Whimsical Woollies is a collection of knit-and-felt patterns arranged into seasons from spring to winter. It contains some of my most tried-and-true, best-selling patterns. Each one has been played with and further embellished, creating new twists and additions, such as my Woolly Gnome and its adaptations.

And finally, this book wouldn't be complete without an extensive embellishing chapter, including all my favorite detailing techniques along with dozens of photos to help

The Art of Knit-and-Felt

Are the patterns included in this book considered needle felting? No, they are what I call "knit-and-felt" patterns. It's the process of throwing a loosely knit 100-percent-wool project into your washing machine to create a shrunken version of its original knit-self. The following chapters will explain the process in great detail, with plenty of how-tos for felting successfully.

Knit-and-felt patterns take much of the guesswork out of felting, as they are designed specifically to achieve the same results again and again. Unlike mistakenly washing your favorite wool sweater and finding that it now fits a child, the results of intentional knit-and-felt projects can be exciting. The possibilities are endless!

stimulate creativity. You will quickly learn I love detail and sharing it with others.

Writing this book has been a wonderful "mind dump," that is, a much-needed opportunity to collect all the fun little details, perfected techniques, and tips I've developed over the years in one spot—*Whimsical Woollies: 20 Projects to Knit and Felt*! The book was written for you, the reader, but selfishly as well for myself. No more notes on little pieces of paper scattered about the house, but a book chock full of details you—and I—can easily refer back to. Happy knitting!

'Cause I Felt Like It:
The Basics of Felting

"The wool fibers expanded and wrapped around each other, locking together and creating a tight fabric through which no winter wind could blow."

–KATHLEEN TAYLOR, *KNIT ONE, FELT TOO*

Felting to me is pure magic. How it transforms from a sloppy, oversized knitted piece into an intentionally shrunken, nubby version of itself is a delight and a real mystery. I believe felting brings out the artist in everyone. Yet felting is both a science and an art.

The science part is simple enough. Wool yarns contain fibers made up of tiny scales. When you place your knitted piece into a wash cycle consisting of hot water, a little soap, and some agitation, a transformation occurs. These little scales open up and loosen when exposed to hot water. They start to tangle themselves onto one another through the agitation process, and then contract and close shut once rinsed in cold water. This results in permanently locked fibers, and there is no going back. The knit fabric has now shrunk to a third of its original size and is much thicker and denser than it was—very unlike its original knitted self.

Every knit-and-felt project starts out as a loosely worked, oversized piece of knitting.

1

Felting White (or Close to White) Wool Yarns

White yarns can be tricky to felt. The manufacturing process for white yarns requires lots of cleaning and bleaching, which strips the wool of its natural oils and may damage or remove the scales that aid in the felting process. In general, the whiter the yarn color, the less likely it will felt. And those that will felt may need more washing and more agitation to felt to the desired size.

That being the case, when you need a white yarn for a felting project, look for one more in the ivory range—the creamier the color, the better it will felt. You can also ask your local yarn stores for their recommendations for what yarns consistently felt. And if you're in doubt about the yarn you've chosen, knit and felt a swatch of it before starting your project. If you wash a swatch three or more times and it hasn't shown signs of shrinkage and/or loss of stitch definition, then it's a good indication that yarn isn't a good choice for felting.

To get you started, here are specific yarns in the worsted white/cream spectrum I've found that felt consistently wash-after-wash:

- Berroco Ultra Alpaca Worsted #6201 Winter White, 50% alpaca/50% wool, 215 yd./198 m per skein
- Brown Sheep Company Nature Spun Worsted #N91 Aran, 100% wool, 245 yd./224 m per skein
- Cascade 220 Worsted #8010 Natural, 100% Peruvian Highland wool, 220 yd./200 m per skein
- Ella Rae Classic Worsted #09 Cream, 100% wool, 219 yd./200 m per skein
- Patons Classic Wool Worsted #201 Winter White and #202 Aran, 100% wool, 210 yd./192 m per skein
- Frog Tree Alpaca Sport #001 Cream, 100% alpaca, 130 yd./119 m per skein (this is a sport weight yarn; two strands knit together will equal the weight of a medium #4 worsted yarn)
- Another fun combination is Cascade 220 Sport #8010 Natural and Frog Tree Alpaca Sport #001 Cream carried together (these two strands knit together will equal the weight of a #4 medium worsted yarn). Yes, you are combining two different yarn brands, which I don't normally recommend, but these two yarns make for wonderful felting partners when a worsted weight is required. The alpaca fills in where the other yarn leaves off!

These cream-colored felted samples show the variation in the nubbiness of texture and the overall ability of these yarns to felt completely and lose original stitch definition.

It Starts with the Yarn

All yarns are not created equally when it comes to the felting process. I recommend using 100 percent wool yarns, but yarn blends containing other animal fibers such as mohair, llama, alpaca, angora, and even silk will felt too. (When felted, these yarns create a fuzzier, hairier, boiled-wool look fabric, perfect for a felted chick or sheep.) Wool yarns that are labeled "superwash" or "machine washable" should be avoided; they will not felt. Yarns containing acrylic also do not felt. These yarns were designed to keep their original shape, and no amount of washing in hot water will change that.

So long as you use the proper yarn, you can use any weight you like. Yarn weights will affect the final size and thickness of the felted piece and how long it may take to felt. Fingering weight yarns will felt quickly and create a thinner final product than worsted weight or bulky yarns.

STICK WITH ONE BRAND PER PROJECT FOR CONSISTENT FELTING

Various yarn brands can felt differently too. Some will felt quickly, while others will require several wash cycles. For example, Cascade 220 tends to felt more slowly than other brands—depending on the color and the weight used, from two to four cycles. On the other hand, Patons Classic Wool yarns felt so quickly, no matter what weight or color, that you need to pay very close attention when felting it, checking on the progress of your project frequently to make sure it doesn't felt (shrink) more than you want it to.

Because of this discrepancy in the way different brands felt, it is important to knit a project in its entirety using the same yarn brand throughout. If you are ever in doubt about how a particular yarn will felt, knit and felt a test swatch before beginning your project. To knit a test swatch of a particular yarn, cast on 20 stitches, knit 30 rows of stockinette, and loosely bind off. Felt the swatch according to the directions that follow. Knitting and felting a test swatch can teach you three things:

1. Whether the specific yarn will even felt.
2. How much it can and will felt.
3. Whether the yarn will hold its color or bleed.

If you use a yarn other than the one I have suggested for a particular project, definitely felt a test swatch to avoid disappointment. (For most of the felting projects in this book, a gauge swatch isn't needed. When it is, the recommended gauge will be indicated.)

Knitting to Felt

Once you have your yarn and know for sure it felts, you are ready to begin knitting your project. But this knitting for the purposes of felting is not knitting as usual.

When knitting for felting, you need to knit loose and big—the sloppier the better. This isn't the time for neat and even stitches. The standard needle size for felting is two to three sizes larger than what the yarn manufacturer recommends for that particular yarn. This information can be found on the wrapper for each skein. For example, the suggested needle sizes for worsted weight yarns are US 7 to 9/4.5 to 5.5 mm. I find that US 10½ or 11/6.5 to 8 mm needles work best for felting worsted weight yarns. This larger needle size coupled with a loose knitting style will create larger stitches and plenty of room for the fibers to shrink down for that boiled-wool look and texture.

Sticking to the Point

Most of the patterns in this book require the use of double-pointed needles (dpns) for knitting in the round because of the small numbers of stitches used. I recommend using wooden dpns rather than metal or aluminum ones. The wooden needles are not as slippery as the metal ones, which helps to hold the stitches on the needles. Wooden dpns come in two lengths: 5 and 7½ inch/13 and 19 cm. All the patterns can be knit using the longer length needles, but a few, like Grade-A Eggs, Chicks, and Ornaments, are more comfortable to knit using the shorter length needles. It helps to keep the knitting fun!

Knitting loosely will likely require a little practice. Resist the impulse to tug on the working yarn at all or to tighten it. Relax your hands. If you find this a struggle, then go up yet another needle size. Remember, the knitted piece, before felting, should look big and loose. It will, in fact, look like bad knitting—and that's okay!

Can a project be knit too large and/or too loose? Yes, in that you might run out of yarn before you're finished and it will take longer to felt overall; but you cannot knit a piece so large and loose that it will not felt properly. Generally, a knitted piece will shrink more in length than it will in width.

Felting by Machine

Felting is a simple process—as simple as throwing the knit piece into your washing machine and turning it on. There are some differences depending on whether you have a front- or top-loading machine (for more details, see below), but in general the process is the same.

Once the piece is knit, place it in a mesh laundry bag large enough to fit the piece comfortably. If possible, use one without a zipper; after several washings, zippers can wear out and break apart. It's also good to have several bags in different sizes to accommodate various sized projects. In the wash, wet wool becomes very heavy, which can cause greater agitation and the opportunity for distortion of its final shape. The purpose of the bag is to help keep the knitted piece compact, not floating around freely in the washer, which will prevent the piece from stretching too much. The mesh bag also keeps any tension on the wet yarn to a minimum, which aids the felting process, and it can reduce the amount of lint left behind in the washer.

The materials needed to felt successfully: a washing machine, mild soap, extra agitation, a mesh laundry bag, a bath towel, and a box of Shout® Color Catchers® (if felting with several yarn color combinations).

Prevent Lint Buildup!

A great way to prevent lint buildup from potentially clogging your sewer or machine's filtering system is to clamp a filter screen (sold in hardware stores) onto your washing machine's water draining hose. This filter gathers the fibers floating in the water and traps them as the water drains out. Be sure to change it periodically so it doesn't get clogged.

Place the mesh bag with your project in the washing machine by itself. I have learned firsthand that you do not want any other fibers in the water with your project. I once threw a worn-out towel in, thinking it would increase the agitation action. What I didn't consider is that all the towel lint would felt into my project and would need to be cut out/off. What a mess!

HOT AND AGITATED

Next, set your machine to fill with the hottest water at the lowest water level possible. Once the machine has filled with water, add a very small amount of soap, just a squirt or two will do. Adding soap helps to further swell the tiny scales, encouraging them to fully open up, and to keep the fibers lubricated while felting. For years I used the same laundry soap I use to wash clothes, and was pleased with the results. I now use the liquid soap Eucalan, which is sold in most yarn stores. It is a gentle, natural lanolin-enriched soap and requires no rinsing. Eucalan is concentrated, so you need only a teaspoon per wash cycle. However, any mild detergent that does not contain bleach will work for felting.

The wash cycle is going to gently agitate your knitted project, but you want to amp up that agitation to make sure those wool fibers open up, mesh, and blend together smoothly. To do that, throw in a pair of old tennis shoes, two or three used tennis balls (not new ones—the fuzz will come off onto your felted project), or a worn pair of jeans. Throw in anything that won't bleed or transfer lint to your felting piece.

The bumpy-edged blue dryer balls found in the Home Essentials section of chain retail stores make great agitators. They come in packs of two. Enlarge the openings slightly with a knife and pitch them into the washer. Making the holes larger will cause the balls to fill with water, adding extra bulk to them and thus creating more agitation and friction.

Never let your piece go through the machine's rinse or spin cycle. Some felters recommend this as part of their felting style/process, but I do not. I have found over the years that in order to obtain the maximum control, especially on my felted figures, it is important to pull the item out before the machine rinses and spins. Doing this prevents further unnecessary felting and the formation of permanent creases and ridges in the felted wool. Even a cold water rinse cycle can further felt a piece.

CHECK IN OFTEN

Each washing machine will felt differently. As the wash cycle progresses, periodically check on the piece to see how it is shrinking. I will check two or three times during the cycle. After felting several times, you will become acquainted with how your machine works with different brands of yarn and colors. Again, if you are ever unsure about a yarn and its felting capability, knit and felt a test swatch to be certain.

After your project has felted for a cycle, take it out, open up the mesh bag, and look at your project. If the knit stitches are still visible, throw it back into the water and reset the wash cycle. It can take up to three or four cycles to completely felt a project, especially if the yarn is light-colored and a heavier weight. There is no magic number of felting cycles, so keep checking on the piece, noting its progress. Err on the side of caution—better to check often than when it's too late; once felted, the size cannot be reversed no matter how much tugging and stretching is exerted upon the piece.

The felting process is considered done when the knitted piece loses the stitch definition and/or has reached its desired size. The projects in this book provide final felted measurements when necessary. Once the size is reached, pull the item out of the washer even if it hasn't finished the wash cycle.

RINSE, SHAPE, AND DRY

Without distorting its shape, gently wring out the excess water, enough to get your item to a sink without much dripping. If a no-rinse soap was used, then no extra rinsing is necessary. Otherwise, gently hand-rinse the felted item in cold water to get the soap out. Rinsing stops the felting process. The cold water closes the fiber's scales. Again, gently wring out the excess water. Wrapping the item in between two towels will help absorb the excess water without further distorting its shape.

The felted piece is now ready for shaping and drying. Tug and pull the piece into the desired shape, rounding out the intended curves and edges. In the case of a pumpkin, you would round out its shape as full as possible. For the figures, you will need to tug and pull them into shape before stuffing them with fiberfill. The fiberfill will hold the wet wool in the desired shape as the sculpture dries. Two-dimensional sculptures like Woolly Leaves need only be tugged into shape and then they're ready for drying. Keep in mind that tugging and pulling a wet piece will increase its finished size by 10 to 15 percent. This will not affect the final sizes of any of the projects in this book.

I will occasionally pin a piece into a desired position. That is, if you want your snowman's scarf to look windswept, pin it up that way. Or I will indent a pumpkin's stem end slightly using a T-pin. Much like blocking a sweater, wet wool will dry as it is positioned.

Allow all felted projects to air dry completely. Wet wool left to slowly dry indoors yields the best results. To dry fully (particularly a stuffed figure) may take two to three days, depending on the amount of humidity in the air. I have sped up the drying process by placing my items on a cookie rack on top of my radiator in the winter months and outside (not in direct sunlight) in the summer. Mesh cookie racks make for perfect drying racks for felted items. A coated cookie rack won't rust, which is particularly helpful for projects made with white yarn (you don't want the rust from an uncoated rack to transfer onto your piece).

If the piece dries and looks misshapen, simply saturate the piece again, gently squeeze out the excess water, tug the item into shape, and allow it to air dry again. This process may require some patience, but it is well worth the effort and time. The rewetting and reshaping process can be applied again and again, even if the piece is stuffed and embellished.

FELTING WITH A TOP-LOADING MACHINE

I have an old top-loader and it has felted faithfully for me over the years. It will be a sad day indeed when that washer cycles for its last time!

To use a top-loading machine for felting, set the dial for the heaviest load (this is a fourteen-minute cycle on my machine), and the hottest and lowest water setting. Top loaders have a central column that helps agitation, but I still throw in two or three dryer balls, tennis shoes, or faded jeans. If I leave the lid open on my machine, the wash cycle automatically stops at the rinse and spin cycle, so I do. Then, if the piece still has stitch definition or the desired size isn't reached, I can reset the machine back to a heavy load and reuse the water again.

If It's Not Felting Enough

Sometimes after three or four wash cycles, the piece will appear to have stopped felting and a significant amount of stitch definition may still be present. When you have used the recommended yarns and followed the felting instructions, it can be frustrating when the piece doesn't felt to the desired shape and size.

To aid this process along, it may be necessary to shock the wool to release the fibers further. Rinse the semi-felted piece in cold water—the colder the better. Cold running water from your sink or a bowl of ice water will do the trick. Then drain the water from the washing machine, throw in the mesh bag with the piece, and reset the machine for a hot and low wash cycle, adding soap again. With this freshened cycle the piece should felt smaller and denser. Carefully watch your piece, though, because the felting may occur quickly, even before the end of the first cycle. If the piece doesn't felt further, then your project is officially done felting. If you're not satisfied with the end result, it's possible that the yarn you've chosen is one that doesn't felt well.

FELTING WITH A FRONT-LOADING MACHINE

The main drawback with a front-loading machine for a felter is that once the machine is turned on, the door cannot be opened, which makes checking on the progress of the felting difficult. On some machines the door can be opened once the water is drained. Read your machine's manual to familiarize yourself with its capabilities.

Set the dial on the front-loader for a half-load or short cycle. Set it for a hot water wash and color rinse cycle. If possible, choose a cycle that doesn't spin at a high speed. Spinning will crease the wool. Some machines have the option to drain the machine without spinning. Read your machine's operating manual to learn its features and what you can or cannot do. Front-loaders don't have a central agitator column, so throw in two or three dryer balls for extra agitation. Again, a worn out pair of tennis shoes or faded jeans will work too.

Run the full cycle if the door can't be opened. Examine the piece for stitch definition and measure for the desired finished size. If it needs more felting, throw the piece back into the washer for a second wash cycle.

FELTING WITH A WONDER WASHER

The Wonder Washer is a portable washing machine that requires no plumbing. I bought mine online. It is made of lightweight plastic and weighs 8.5 pounds. It's the perfect size for washing and felting on a kitchen countertop.

The Wonder Washer shown with its bucket atop its motor. It is now ready for washing or felting in any room, any time. The Wonder Washer's motor section and cord fit completely inside the washing bucket for easier storage and transportation.

Pour the hottest water possible from your kitchen sink into the Wonder Washer and add a little soap like Eucalan or a gentle fabric detergent. Set the dial to begin the wash cycle. Each cycle runs for about fifteen minutes. A typical felting project can take one to three cycles, again depending on the yarn used. Like a front-loader, the Wonder Washer does not have an internal agitating column, so add two to three blue dryer balls or tennis balls for extra agitation. The Wonder Washer also doesn't have a rinse or spin cycle, so when the felting is complete, pour the water out into the sink. Rinse the piece under cold water and gently squeeze out the excess. The Wonder Washer works best for smaller projects like the Vintage-Style Ball Ornaments and the Baby Chick. Like the top- and front-loading machines, if the project isn't felting like you want after several rounds, cold shock the piece as directed in If It's Not Felting Enough (page 6).

Felting by Hand

Hand felting isn't an option for every project, particularly larger ones. It can be tiresome for the arms and is slow going. However, for a few of the projects and their individual pieces in this book, hand felting is recommended, as you need to have precise control over the sizing. Also, any felting project knit using fingering weight yarns will be easiest to felt by hand because of its initial size.

To begin, in your kitchen sink, wet the knit item under hot running water, adding a squirt of soap. Wearing rubber gloves for this is a good idea, as the gloves will protect your hands from the hot water and aid in the agitation process, especially if the gloves have textured palms.

You want to alternate between putting the item under the hottest water and rubbing it between your palms. If needed, add more soap. The more you rub the item under the water, the more the soap rinses out. Adding more soap keeps the piece smooth and lubricated. Felting is complete when the finished piece is about a third to half of its original size, even if you can still see the knit stitches.

If the piece seems to be taking a long time to shrink down, it may need a little assistance. Immerse the item in a bowl of ice water to shock the fibers. Pull it out of the water and start the hand felting process again.

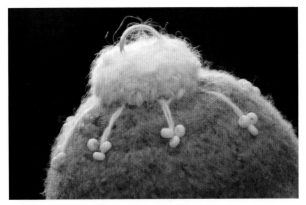

Little projects like the Vintage-Style Ball Ornaments hanger caps are the perfect size for the hand-felting process. Hand felting gives you greater control to ensure the item fits accurately.

In conclusion, felting by machine or by hand is a simple process once you get the hang of it. Your success comes through practice and learning firsthand these techniques and what yarns felt best. Like any new hobby or skill, you need to start somewhere, and a little practice goes a long way. The desired result is a textured surface screaming to you, "Embellish me!" Embellishing is all about adding further detailing to your finished surface. In the next chapter you'll find tutorials on my favorite embellishing techniques and everything you'll need to know for adding that detail to the projects in this book.

Color Bleeding

Bleeding can occur when darker color yarns (particularly red) are washed in hot water. If your knitted piece is all red and it bleeds into the hot water, it really doesn't matter. But when a piece is knit using both light and dark colored yarns, it is critical to minimize the possibility of bleeding.

I have found Shout® Color Catcher® sheets, available in the laundry section of the supermarket, to be very effective. These dye-trapping sheets absorb the dyes released into the hot water and prevent yarn colors from bleeding onto one another. Throw one to two sheets or a similar product into the machine along with the knitted piece.

In a project like the St. Nick Gnome, with its skin tone face and red hat, one to two sheets will keep the red dye from turning the skin color pinkish. Some bleeding may still occur, but it will be slight in comparison to what it would be if the sheets weren't used.

Making the Project Bigger or Smaller

Each project in this book can be knit and felted as noted in the pattern, or be made smaller or larger. To change the size of the final project, use a yarn of a finer or heavier weight and adjust your needle size.

For example, the felted Harvest Pumpkins pattern uses a #4 medium worsted weight yarn and US size 10^1/$_2$/6.5 mm needles, which are two sizes larger than the recommended size for that weight of yarn. If you'd like the pumpkin smaller, knit it up in a #1 super fine (sock or fingering) yarn with US size 5/3.75 mm needles or in #2 fine (baby or sport) or #3 light worsted (DK or light worsted) weight yarn with size US 8/5 mm needles. If you'd like the pumpkin to be bigger, try using a feltable #5 bulky or #6 super bulky weight yarn with US size 13 or 15/9 or 10 mm needles.

Some yarn brands (like Cascade 220 or Brown Sheep Company's Nature Spun) offer the same colors in different weights, which is very helpful if you want a set of projects with the same color scheme but in different sizes.

The following chart shows the various yarn weights with the appropriate size needles to use when you are knitting to felt. Use this chart as a reference when selecting yarns throughout this book.

Needle Sizes to Use When Knitting to Felt

Yarn Weight	Needle Size
#1 Super fine (sock, fingering)	US 5/3.75 mm
#2 Fine (sport)	US 8/5 mm
#3 or #4 Light or Medium (DK or worsted)	US 10^1/$_2$/6.5 mm
#5 Bulky (chunky)	US 13/9 mm

Keep in mind that if you adjust the size of a project, the embellishing details will need to be adjusted as well. For example, if making a smaller or larger gnome, the nose, eyes, and beard length will need to be adjusted to an appropriate size to fit the face.

All the Harvest Pumpkins shown here were knit using exactly the same pattern. Simply changing the yarn weight and needle sizes for each will transform the final size.

Knitting Abbreviations and Terms

beg — Beginning.

BO — Bind off.

CO — Cast on.

dpn(s) — Double-pointed needle(s).

I-cord — On a double-pointed needle, cast on the desired number of stitches and knit. *Never turn the work.* Slide the stitches to the right end of the needle and knit again. Repeat until the I-cord is the desired length.

inc 1 — Increase one stitch by knitting into the front and then into the back of the same stitch.

k2tog — Knit two stitches together through their front loops; this creates a right-slanting decrease.

k2togTBL — Knit two stitches together through their back loops; this creates a left-slanting decrease.

knit side — The side of the knitted piece with the knit stitches facing out.

kwise — Knitwise; as if to knit.

M1 — Increase one stitch by making a loop cast-on onto the right-hand needle.

p2tog — Purl two stitches together through the front loops; this creates a right-slanting decrease on the knit side.

p2togTBL — Purl two stitches together through the back loops. Slip the two stitches knitwise, one at a time, to the right needle. Return these stitches to the left needle, keeping them twisted. Then purl the two stitches together through the back loops, creating a right-slanting decrease on the knit side.

p3tog — Purl three stitches together through the front loops; this creates a right-slanting decrease on the knit side.

psso — Pass a slipped stitch over the just knitted or purled stitch and off the right-hand needle; this creates a left-slanting decrease.

pwise — Purlwise; as if to purl.

rnd(s) — Round(s).

sl 1 — Slip one stitch as if to knit.

ssk — Slip, slip, knit. Slip one stitch as if to knit onto the right needle, and then slip another in the same way. Insert the left needle into the front of the two slipped stitches. Knit these stitches together; this creates a left-slanting decrease.

stockinette st — Knit one row, turn the work, and purl back. Continue in this manner.

st(s) — Stitch(es).

to — Everything between the first * and the second is to be repeated as directed in the pattern.

turn work — After working a row or round, flip the work around to the other side (knit or purl), and with the working yarn attached to the left needle start knitting or purling as the pattern indicates. Turn works are necessary in the pattern design for overall shaping of the final piece.

w&t (k) — Wrap & turn knit side. Knit up to the turning point, slip the next stitch purlwise onto the right needle, bring the yarn forward between the needles, return the slipped stitch to the left needle, pass the yarn between the needles to the back of the work, turn work to the purl side, and begin purling.

w&t (p) — Wrap & turn purl side. Purl up to the turning point, slip the next stitch purlwise onto the right needle, bring the yarn to the back between the needles, return the slipped stitch to the left needle, pass the yarn between the needles to the front of the work, turn work to the knit side, and begin knitting.

yo — Yarn over. A yarn over produces an intentional hole within your knitting. Bring the yarn between the needles to the front of the right needle, and then to the back to prepare it for knitting the next stitch.

For the Love of Detail:
Embellishing

Embellishing is an exciting way to add detail and personality to any felted project. I fell into embellishing quite by accident as a means to fix a mistake I had made while felting.

Several years ago, I taught a felted bag class. A few days before the class, I was hurrying to get the bag felted. I had thrown it into the washing machine and gone to help my husband paint the living room. Of course, I totally forgot about the bag. It had gone through the wash, rinse, and spin cycles and ended up several inches smaller than it should have been. Yikes! I didn't have time to knit and felt another. I was a new and nervous teacher, and too insecure to admit my felting mistake. So, being the problem solver I am, I embellished the bag.

First, I cut out small squares from a felted wool sweater I had. I embroidered them onto the bag with a blanket stitch (the only stitch I knew back then). I taught myself the feather stitch and added a few gold buttons that I had found in an antique store. In the end, I had created a sweet little one-of-a-kind work of art. Not one student noticed the bag's rather small size!

This "mistake" taught me a valuable lesson: There are no felting mistakes, only felting opportunities to learn from. Embellishments will shift the eye away from the mistake only you know about. The eye is naturally drawn to the top layer of any felted project, focusing on any embroidery, needle felting, and/or button and bead detailing you add.

Embellishing makes each felted piece unique. It allows you to take the same simple pattern and create dozens of one-of-a-kind pieces. No two items ever need be alike.

Each of the techniques I cover in this chapter—whether added before or after felting—can become a layer of detail in your project, building in sequential order on top of one another. For example, Grade-A Eggs can

My first official attempt at embellishing a felted bag—a functional, one-of-a-kind work of art!

be knit using several yarn colors to create stripes. Once felted, it can be embroidered to add more detail and color. Beads can then be sewn about the egg for tiny polka dots of color and texture.

Each technique in this chapter begins with a description of the method and the materials needed. How-to instructions, photos, and/or illustrations follow with further design suggestions. By no means is the list of techniques exhaustive, but it will expand your embellishing world.

Embellishing requires some practice, patience, and a willingness to play and experiment. Pick at least one technique outlined in this chapter and apply it to one or several of your projects. A simple embroidered stitch design will carry your creativity a long way. And remember that embellishing doesn't have to be permanent. Appliqués, beads, sequins, buttons, and embroidery can be easily repositioned or removed if you don't like the result.

All the projects in this book can be embellished as little or as much as you choose. Then be ready for the chorus of "oohs" and "ahs" to follow.

Start an Inspiration Station

When my children were small I didn't get out much, so I started collecting catalogs as a means to stimulate my creativity. Hanna Andersson, Pottery Barn, Crate & Barrel, and even J. Jill had catalog pages filled with color combinations for baby sweaters, whimsical decorating ideas for my house, and seasonal DIY ornaments to make. These catalogs became a means to aid me in adding fun detailing to my kids' mittens or a simple accent or trim for their sweaters—all could be duplicated in my own color scheme and style for my knitted projects. I began tearing out pages and filing them away in a paper folder for future reference.

This folder now overflows with little bits of inspiration, a priceless treasure chest of creativity. When I need a fresh idea, I flip through my Inspiration-Station folder, looking for a little something to spark an idea, to get me started. This folder has never let me down!

Create your own Inspiration-Station folder. It's as simple as paging through a catalog or magazine with an eye for whimsical design opportunities. Don't censor yourself—if something attracts you, rip it out and put it in the folder. It could be some small detail of a larger design that you don't even particularly like that leads you to a fresh idea.

Color My World: Knitting in Color

The first line of embellishment in felting is to knit the project in one or a combination of colors. But choosing yarn colors and making color combinations can seem like a gigantic leap of faith, particularly when the project will be felted. You may ask yourself: Do these colors complement one another? How might these colors blend after felting together? Will I like the felted end result? Here are two simple suggestions to help ease the color selection process.

Go yarn shopping with a young child. Ask her or him to pick out two to three colors from within the designated yarn brand. Kids will pick colors they like. They are not

hindered by the "rules" that inhibit and govern adults. They choose colors according to their hearts not their heads. The best compliments I've received are on knitting projects that my kids had picked the yarn colors for.

If shopping with kids isn't your thing, then borrow this idea from the experts: Take along fabric swatches you like. Fabric designers choose and combine colors all day long. Browse through the endless fabric choices that quilt and upholstery stores have to offer, pick out fabrics with color combinations, tones, and hues that speak to you, and buy a quarter yard of each. Then the next time you go yarn shopping, bring these fabric swatches with you and choose yarn colors using the swatches as your reference.

KNIT ONE, STRIPE TWO

Stripes are added to your project as you knit and can provide visual interest and whimsy to any piece, with little need for extra embellishing post-felting. When selecting colors for striping, keep in mind that yarn weights and brands can felt differently, so be sure that the colors you choose for a particular project are all of the same weight and brand.

For the best results when felting, each stripe should be at least two or more rows or rounds deep. A single row or round of color will felt into a thin line and can disappear, especially if a light-colored yarn is used. Your stripes can all be of the same depth or you can add further interest by having stripes of varying thicknesses. After felting a project with stripes, I sometimes like to add embroidery accents, like the feather or the chain stitch, where the different-colored stripes meet. This adds another layer of striping, color, and texture.

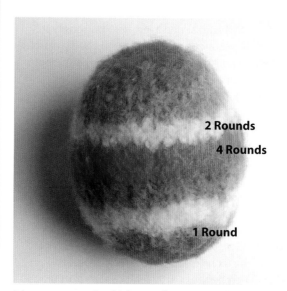

2 Rounds

4 Rounds

1 Round

It's easy to vary the thickness of your stripes by knitting one or more rounds of each color.

Always begin a new stripe color at the beginning of a row or round. There is no need to break the yarn with each color change. You can loosely carry the yarn up the knitting between color changes. Before felting a striped project, secure all loose ends and seal any holes resulting from the addition of the new yarn colors.

A SPECKLED LOOK

You can create a speckled effect in the finished felted fabric by knitting the project with two or even three yarns held together at the same time. Speckling adds a second or even a third accent color to the felted project. Speckling is similar to variegation, but more random in how it melds after felting. For this technique, it doesn't matter whether the yarns knit together are the same weight, but to ensure consistent felting, use yarns from the same brand.

The combination of yarn colors knit in this way will soften and blend with felting. To create a subtle color combination, the main color should be a worsted weight yarn and the second color a similar tone in a sport weight yarn—for example, a brown worsted weight yarn and a tan sport weight yarn. These colors will meld together to create a fabric a shade or two lighter than the original brown. To create a bolder effect, use two contrasting colors of the same yarn weight, such as red and yellow worsted weight yarns. These two colors will meld but still retain their identity, with bursts of each color throughout the felted project. When in doubt about a color combination and how it will felt, knit and felt a swatch to test it.

Needle Me This: Needle Felting

Winding vines, simple curls, and shape cutouts from acrylic or wool felt, wool roving, and scraps of yarn are easily attached to any project by means of needle felting. The felting needle, as it pokes, breaks down the fibers of these mediums (much like the added agitation produced from the dryer balls does when the knitted fabric is being felted in the washer), melding them with the felted wool of your project to create a seamless look, like a painting created in wool.

For this technique, you need a felting needle, a foam pad to work on, and the stuff that gives needle felting its purpose: pieces of acrylic or wool felt cut into shapes, scraps of yarn in various weights, and/or pinches of wool roving (cleaned and carded fleece, in its natural color or dyed). Yarn stores sell most of these supplies, and all of them are available online. Many yarn stores sell needle felting kits, complete with a variety of felting needles, a foam pad, and how-to instructions—some kits even

This Harvest Pumpkin was knit carrying two worsted weight yarns together, an orange and a gold, to create the random, variegated look throughout the pumpkin's body.

The poinsettia flower was needle felted onto this ornament after it was felted and stuffed. White and green wool roving were used to form the flower. The curls and vines are needle felted from lengths of fine yarn. French knots and seed beads were added for texture and further detail in the flower's center.

include several small rolls of roving. These are perfect for the beginner needle felter.

FELTING NEEDLES

Needle felting is accomplished using a special barbed needle. Felting needles come in a range of sizes (referred to as *gauge*)—the higher the gauge number, the finer the needle and the smaller the hole it will leave in your work. A size 38-gauge felting needle is primarily used to baste and to adhere felt pieces, wool roving, and yarn to your felted project. I refer to this gauge needle as an "all-purpose" felting needle throughout this book. Basting tacks the pieces into position so you can see if you like the way they look before permanently adhering them. I use a 40-gauge needle for more delicate work, like adding the jack-o'-lantern face to the Harvest Pumpkin on page 84. The 38- and 40-gauge felting needles will cover the majority of the needle felting work called for in this book.

FOAM PAD

The foam pad protects your table or lap from the sharp point of the felting needle. The pad should be at least 1 inch/2.5 cm thick and made of high-density foam. Fabric stores will often cut them to any size you like.

Most of the felted projects in this book are stuffed with fiberfill and require no foam pad when needle felting, as the stuffed figure itself functions as the foam pad. But for flat projects like the Autumn Leaves (page 70), a foam pad is needed, and it should be large enough to fit the entire leaf. A pad is also needed when sculpting three-dimensional shapes with wool roving. The nose and chin for Matilda the Witch are sculpted from green roving first on top of a foam pad, and then attached to her face.

When needle felting with roving, little hairy remnants will inevitably be left behind on the pad. To minimize the effect of color mixing, you should have multiple pads: one reserved for needle felting with light colors, another for dark colors, and perhaps a third for those colors in between. This is especially important when working with white and cream-colored roving.

NEEDLE FELTING ACRYLIC AND WOOL FELT

Purchased felt can be made from wool, acrylic, or a combination of the two. The cut edges of felt won't fray, making it an ideal medium for embellishing. Felt details can be attached to your project using needle felting and/or appliqué embroidery.

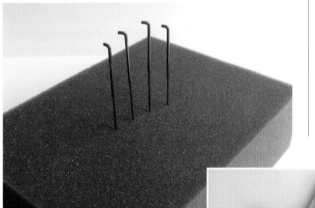

A foam pad and a set of felting needles are all you need to begin your needle-felting adventure!

The four squares on the left are wool blend felt. They are warmer in hue compared to the acrylic squares in similar green tones on the right. Similar colors in acrylic felt are usually brighter in hue and tone than in wool.

Acrylic felt: Acrylic felt is sold in 9 x 12 in./23 x 30.5 cm sheets in craft stores and is ideal for cutting out shapes to be needle felted onto your project. It is inexpensive and available in endless colors and a few patterns—why not buy a sheet in every color!

I recommend washing acrylic felt before using it. This will eliminate some of its plastic sheen and stiffness, softening it and giving its surface the appearance of wool. Washing it will not shrink the felt.

To hand wash a piece of felt, wet it under the hot water from your sink along with a little soap. Scrub the felt between your hands for about a minute. Rinse in cold water to get the soap out. Wring out the excess water and blot dry between towels. Smooth out any wrinkles, and then allow the felt to air dry completely. Once dry, the felt is ready to be cut into various shapes and attached to your felted project.

Wool felt: Wool felt (available as 100 percent wool or as a wool blend in combination with rayon) also comes in 9 x 12 inch sheets in a variety of colors, its colors warmer in hue than those of acrylic. Wool felt is thicker and has a denser texture than acrylic felt. Light won't shine through a wool felt sheet as it will with an acrylic one. This denseness makes wool felt ideal for appliqué designs. It is slightly more expensive than acrylic felt, but still affordable. It can be found in quilt/fabric stores as well as online. Some stores sell it by the yard. Wool felt doesn't need washing beforehand; it can be cut into shapes and immediately adhered to your project.

Attaching Felt to Your Project

Needle felting and embroidery are the two main techniques used to attach felt shapes to a felted wool project.

Decide what shapes you'd like to use. Cookie cutters in all shapes and sizes can function as templates. Place one on a sheet of paper, trace around the cutter, then cut the template out. Pin the paper template to a piece of felt and cut the shape out with a pair of scissors. If you want to create polka dots, use coins to create different sizes. The actual coins can be used as templates; place a coin on a piece of felt and, using sharp scissors, cut around the coin. Then position the cut shapes on top of your wool project and baste them into place using needle felting. Needle-felted basting lightly holds the felt piece in place and replaces the need for pins. If you change your mind on placement, the piece can still be lifted up and moved to a new position. Using a felting needle (if it's a small felt piece, use a 40-gauge needle; otherwise, use a 38-gauge needle), first baste the piece into place. To do this, poke the needle through the felt piece in just a few spots to tack it into place on the felted fabric underneath. Do this with all the felt pieces you intend to use. Now take a look and see if their positioning pleases you. If you want to

A simple jack-o'-lantern face, whether spooky or jolly, is quick work with little acrylic felt cutouts and a felting needle!

move some or all of them, it's easy to pull the felt pieces away and reposition.

Once you're happy with the positioning, begin poking the piece, especially the outer edges, until they are firmly in place. Keep poking until the piece of felt lies smooth and flat against the felted wool beneath. The more you poke with the needle, the more the felt adheres to the wool underneath. Repeat this with all the pieces. Once completed, lightly wet each piece and a soft toothbrush with water. Gently brush the felt surface, adding more water if needed. The water and brushing will soften and blend the felt with the wool base and eliminate any holes left behind by the felting needle. I only wet and brush projects that are adhered by needle felting alone.

Acrylic felt, because it is thin, will break down quicker when needle felted and will lie flat and smooth against the wool beneath it, giving the look of being knitted into the felt. Wool felt is thicker and will sit slightly on top of the wool beneath. To decoratively soften the felt edges, you can also embroider the needle-felted piece afterward with decorative stitching. When working with wool felt and especially with projects that will be handled a great deal, I recommend using this combination of needle felting and embroidery to firmly adhere felt pieces to your project.

NEEDLE FELTING WOOL ROVING

Roving is cleaned and carded sheep's wool. It is sold in half-ounce or larger packages, dyed or in its natural color. You can find it in local yarn stores and online. Roving vendors also sell variety packs in a wide range of hues, from spring-like pastels, to vibrant colors, to earth tones like gray, heathery brown, and cream. Local wool and sheep festivals are a great venue for picking up hand-dyed rovings in unusual colors and textures.

Using a felting needle and roving, you can create designs directly on your felted project. With a little practice, these designs can have great detailing, shading, and depth.

Polka Dots

If you've never needle felted with roving before, start simple, with small polka dots. Pull off a pinch of roving. Wet the palm of one hand with a little saliva and roll the roving between your palms to form a tiny ball. (Wetting the roving will help it keep its ball-like shape as you begin needle felting.) The size of the polka dot will be determined by the amount of roving you use and the amount of rolling you do. Rolling the roving between your hands creates a denser, smaller polka dot compared to if you don't roll at all. A denser ball of roving will hold its shape better when poked by the felting needle.

Position the ball of roving on the wool project. With the felting needle, poke the roving into the wool's surface, basting it first and then flattening it into a round dot. Poke along the outer edges to form a round dot. Wherever you poke the roving it will indent slightly, so round out the dot's edges to be more ball-like. The ball of roving can be flattened completely or left slightly raised.

To finish, wet your index finger with water and smooth it over the roving. This will blend the flattened roving with the wool underneath and eliminate any holes the felting needle left behind.

Design Detail: Sew a seed bead into the center of a polka dot made from roving to create a dot within a dot. This is a great way to add little bursts of additional color throughout your project.

Freeform Designs

Wool roving can also be used to create needle-felted freeform pictorial designs that, in their transparency, will look like they were painted onto your felted wool projects with watercolors. The best way to learn how to do this is through doing, experimenting with layering different colored rovings on top of one another or creating shading by building up color in areas using more roving and then lightening the shade by using less. You can create incredible detail and depth doing this, to the point that your design can look almost photographic.

White roving polka dots turn this woolly mushroom into a whimsical woodland toadstool ready to be discovered amongst the leaves of a potted plant.

The small pink and large blue flowers were needle felted with wool roving. Embroidery and beads were then added to create texture, shading, and further detailing.

NEEDLE FELTING YARN SCRAPS

Yarn scraps of any weight can be used in needle felting. The yarn doesn't need to be 100 percent wool, but it is preferred. Yarn scraps are perfect for creating vines, squiggles, or curlicues, or to write your child's name on his or her Crazy Quilt Holiday Stocking (page 96). Use a fingering weight yarn for a thin line or a bulkier weight yarn for a thicker one.

Wool yarn scraps (100 percent wool or blended wools) can also be turned into roving by first cutting them into 1-inch/2.5-cm pieces and then pulling the plies apart. Now rub the plies between your fingers to create little bits of yarn roving. You can then roll those bits together between your palms into bigger balls. The yarn roving is then attached to your project using an all-purpose (38-gauge) felting needle. Using wool yarn scraps is a great way to coordinate the embellishing, using the same yarns that the project was knit and felted with. These bits of same-colored roving are ideal for covering over stitched seams to blend with the wool underneath and for quickly covering up or correcting holes and felting mishaps when needed.

Curlicues

Any weight of wool yarn can be used for this. Fingering and sport weight yarns create thinner curls and worsted

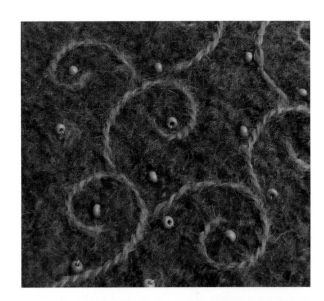

I love experimenting with color palettes. Here I took a minimal approach, limiting the colors of the felted project and its embellishment to shades of blue and cream. Use the same yarns you knit your project with and coordinate them in creating polka dots and embroidery stitching all done in the same color palette.

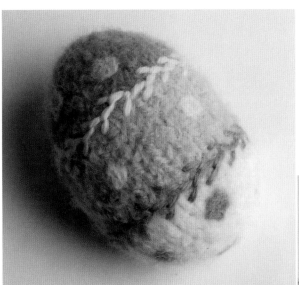

Right: *Another thing you can do with yarn scraps is create whimsical curls, like those on this sheep. Fool your friends into thinking you spent endless hours embroidering this simple design!*

Above right: *French knots or seed beads can be sewn randomly about the curls to add additional texture and bursts of color. To create the French knots, use the same yarn that was used to needle felt the curls.*

and bulky weights create thicker ones. Cut several 4-inch/10-cm lengths of any weight wool yarn. Lay one strand of yarn onto your project, positioning it into a curl. Starting at one end of the yarn, begin lightly poking it with a 38-gauge felting needle to baste the yarn into position. Next, place another strand of yarn so one end butts up to the newly basted curl. Baste this strand into a curl. Basting the piece into position allows you to see how the design will look before you commit to permanently adhering it to the wool underneath. Continue this process of basting the yarns until the whole area is covered in curlicues. Vary the curls so some turn to the right and some to the left.

After all the curls are basted into position, adhere them permanently to your project by needle felting over them all again. The more the yarn is poked, the flatter it becomes, but eventually the yarn will regain its original twisted-ply look.

Squiggles and Wavy Lines

Use the same method as for the curlicues to create vines or any kind of freeform squiggle design you choose (you can also use this method for monogramming a piece). Leaving the yarn attached to the skein, pin the loose end to your wool project with a straight pin and then continue to pin the yarn in place in the design you want. Do not cut the yarn until you are all done basting it into position. The yarn length will shrink up some the more you poke, so you don't want to cut it too soon.

With the felting needle, baste the entire length of yarn to your wool project. Adjust the loops along the way if needed. Continue to needle felt the yarn until it lies smooth and flat and is adhered to the wool underneath. To create one continuous line that wraps around your project (I like doing this on Grade-A Eggs and Vintage-Style Ball Ornaments), overlap the loose ends at the back and poke them until they visibly blend together, then snip the yarn end and poke it until smooth and flat.

Felt Like It: Appliqué

Appliqué refers to attaching decorative cutout shapes to your felted project using embroidery. To appliqué, you will need wool felt (100 percent or a wool blend) in various colors (wool felt is recommended for appliqué because of its thicker texture and how it rests on top of the wool), a chenille needle (size 24), and embroidery floss. Pearl cotton, a twisted cotton thread, in either size 8 or 12 is preferred for appliqué.

Trace and cut out the desired shapes from the felt. You will attach these shapes to your felted project using either the blanket stitch or the overhand stitch (see page

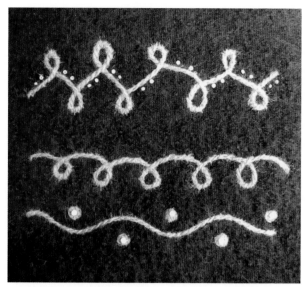

Create vines that squiggle all over the wool. Embroider French knots or sew seed beads along the vine to create berries. Small polka dots made from wool or yarn roving can be needle felted along the squiggly lines for additional detailing.

You can create whimsical folk art dots using wool felt and simple embroidery to achieve a variety of designs.

20 or 22). Choose floss colors that will coordinate and complement your wool felt pieces and not distract. Floss that is similar in color to the felt will blend and most likely disappear. Select a color that is one to two shades lighter or darker than the felt. To help with color selection, take the felt pieces along when shopping for the floss.

To create finer embroidery stitches when using DMC floss, the plies of the thread can be pulled apart into two strands of three plies each, then use only one of these strands. Use a three-ply strand for creating finer, more delicate stitches that are mainly decorative in nature, such as for the veins on a green felt leaf. Embroidering with all six plies of cotton floss or the twisted pearl cotton thread creates a stronger, bolder color against the wool felt and thicker and stronger stitches to adhere the felt to the wool underneath.

Insert the needle into the bottom of the wool project, coming up in the position of your first felt piece. Anchor the floss to the wool underneath by sewing a tiny stitch where the floss emerges. Embroider the felt to the project using the blanket stitch or a series of straight stitches such as the overhand stitch. To finish, bury the end within the wool or come out the bottom, secure the stitch, and snip all loose ends.

Stitch It, Stitch It Good: Embroidery

Embroidery adds additional color and texture to your almost finished piece. Think of your felted wool piece as the canvas for further embellishment with embroidery. This section includes instructions for eight embroidery stitches. Practice and perfect several of these stitches, and you will find them to be your go-to stitches every time.

GETTING STARTED

With the purchase of just a few supplies, you'll be embroidering in no time.

Chenille Needle

The chenille needle is a short, sharp-end needle with an eye big enough to fit either embroidery floss or fingering and sport weight yarns, and even some worsted weights. The needle's sharp tip allows you to embroider on top of the wool and in those hard-to-reach areas. This means the embroidery can be worked completely on top of your piece without having to have access to the bottom side of your project. This is necessary especially when working on projects that are stuffed and sewn shut, like most of the sculptures in this book.

Embroidery Threads

To create an all-wool look to your project, select either fingering or sport weight wool yarns. Fingering weight yarns create finer embroidery stitches as compared to thicker yarns.

DMC cotton floss is another choice for embroidery thread. Cotton floss adds a slight sheen and brightness to

your wool project. Combining mediums like cotton floss with wool yarns creates interest and whimsy. With DMC floss, the color choices are endless. For example, there are dozens of shades of the color green to choose from. DMC floss is made up of six single strands that can easily be separated so you can adjust the thickness of your stitches. Using all six plies will create a thicker stitch. The plies can be pulled apart to create thinner strands, thus finer stitches. Don't use fewer than three plies; otherwise your stitches will likely get lost in the felted wool's thick texture.

Another thread option is pearl cotton, which is twisted and so tightly woven that you can't divide its strands like you can with DMC cotton floss. This quality adds a slightly thicker texture to your embroidery right away. Pearl cotton comes in several thicknesses. The most popular (and thickest) size sold in craft stores is 5. Sizes 8 and 12 are preferred when embroidering on wool appliqués. Look for sizes 8 and 12 pearl cotton in embroidery/cross-stitching stores and online. The size 8 pearl cotton is equivalent to

Shown are four options of embroidery threads, starting from the bottom left: DMC cotton floss, pearl cotton (size 5), a ball of pearl cotton (size 8), and a skein of wool fingering weight yarn. All are cream colored, but each would add a different texture and sheen to your embroidery project.

three strands of regular cotton embroidery floss, and size 12 is equivalent to one to two strands. Remember, the higher the number, the finer the thread will appear.

ANCHORING STITCHES

To begin any embroidery project on wool, you need to first anchor the thread to your project. Thread the chenille needle with the yarn or floss. Come up from the bottom of the work and insert the needle through the wool. Where the thread emerges, sew a tiny, anchoring stitch to secure the thread to the felt. This stitch will be concealed once you begin embroidering. If you can't come up from the bottom of your work (the piece may be too small for your fingers to get into or if the item is a stuffed sculpture), insert the threaded needle through the wool about 2 inches away from where you want to begin stitching and then come out in the position to begin stitching. Pull the thread just until the tail disappears within the wool. Where the needle emerges, sew a tiny stitch here to anchor the thread.

It's time to learn those basic stitches, and watch your embellishing abilities start to blossom and grow!

BLANKET STITCH

The blanket stitch is traditionally used along the outside edge of a fabric. It is decorative but also functional, as it can be used to sew two fabric pieces together. The arms of this stitch should be the same length within a project,

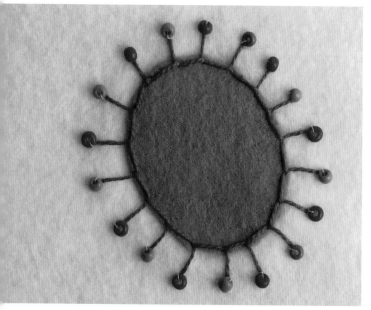

Embroidering the blanket stitch in a circle pattern creates a decorative edge to any round roving or felt cutout. You can add a French knot or seed bead at the end of each stitch's arm.

I Need More Help!

The web is a great resource to learn more about embroidery. My favorite resource is Mary Corbet's Needle 'n Thread website, needlenthread.com. It gives plenty of tips, tricks, and resources for all your hand embroidery needs. It also includes a full array of how-to videos on just about every embroidery stitch you'll ever require.

but from project to project you can vary their length to suit what you are doing. Practice this stitch, working to achieve a consistent stitch length.

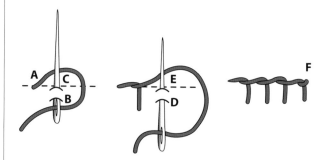

Come up from the bottom of your work at A, and stitch from B to C. Keeping the thread under the chenille needle, pull it through the wool. Moving to the right, stitch from D to E. Repeat for desired length. To finish, tack the yarn down at the edge of the line, F.

CHAIN STITCH

The chain stitch creates a line consisting of a series of little links. This stitch can be used to add colorful stripes on top of the felted wool or to separate two blocks of color with a thinner, decorative stripe. The chain stitch can also be worked into curves and curls.

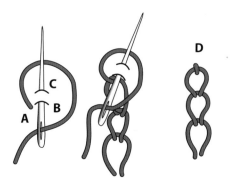

Come up from the bottom of your work at A. Direct the chenille needle from B to C. Wrap the yarn behind the

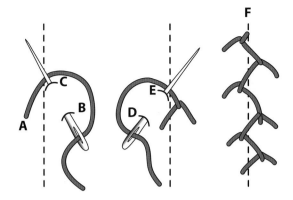

Embroider two chain stitches, side by side, coming out from the same spot, to create dainty little leaves. Place a second color French knot or seed bead between each leaf chain as a tiny flower head.

needle from left to right. Be consistent in wrapping the yarn the same way each time, so the chain doesn't become twisted. Pull the needle through. Repeat this sequence for the desired length. To finish, tack the yarn at the end of the chain, D.

FEATHER STITCH

Use the feather stitch to create wandering vines and twig-like branches that zigzag about your felted piece. It can also be used to decoratively separate two blocks of colors.

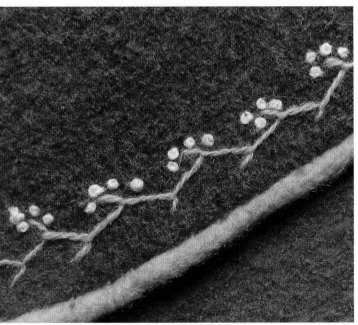

Use the feather stitch to create twig-like branches and create little berries along the vine by embroidering French knots or sewing on seed beads.

Come up from the bottom of your work at A. Working along an imaginary line, direct the chenille needle from B to C, and then from D to E. Repeat for the desired length, creating continuous arms on either side of the imaginary line: one arm coming from the right and then the next from the left side. To finish, tack the yarn down at the end of the last stitch, F.

FRENCH KNOTS

French knots create little rose-like stitches. They can be used singularly to create a little flower head or berry along an embroidered vine or collectively to fill an area. French knots add wonderful texture. If French knots turn out not to be your thing, seed beads can be exchanged in any project instead.

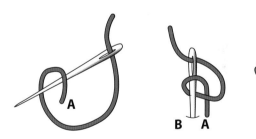

Come up from the bottom of your work at A. Wrap the yarn around the needle two to three times and bring the needle back down through the wool at B, closest to A as possible. Keep the thread taut as the needle is directed to the next knot position. To create larger knots, use a thicker yarn or wrap the yarn three times.

Through the years I have discovered a helpful trick to achieve consistent French knots every time. After you have wrapped the yarn around your needle, and as you slowly pull the thread to form the knot, the thread will begin to form a circle. When this circle gets to be about a silver dollar size, lay the needle down and pick up the two sides of the circle, one side with your left hand and the other with your right. Gently pull each end, tightening the knot against the wool. Don't tighten too much, or you

Pull each end of the loop so the knot rests snugly against the wool, but not so tightly that the ends don't glide through the knot when pulled.

Another helpful technique if you're having trouble keeping your French knots consistent and similar in size is to use a felting needle to lightly poke the knots into perfection.

won't be able to pull the threads through to finish the knot. Now pick up the needle again and pull the attached thread. The threads will pull through the knot and rest on top of it evenly every time!

OVERHAND STITCH

The overhand stitch is used to appliqué cutouts to your wool project. The stitch hugs the felt piece and decoratively adheres it to the wool underneath.

Come up from the bottom of your work and, starting from the outer edge of the cutout, direct the needle into the felt about ⅛ to ¼ inch/.3 to .6 cm away. Then direct the needle back to the outer edge and into the wool underneath; continue to evenly repeat around the entire felt piece shape as needed.

The overhand stitch, shown around the edges of the leaf and flower center, adds simple but functional detailing.

LONG-STEM FLY STITCH

The long-stem fly stitch creates a Y-shaped stitch whose arm length can be adjusted to each specific project.

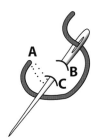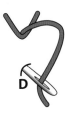

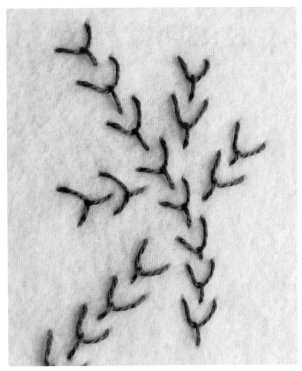

Come up from the bottom of your work at A. If you are unable to come up from the bottom of your work, such as with the sheep pattern, then direct your threaded needle into the top of the wool about 2 inches/15 cm from A, and come out at A. Direct your needle into B and then into C, making sure the thread is under your needle as you pull the thread. To finish, create a longer stitch to tack the end down, D. To complete, direct the needle into the wool and come back out several inches away from your ending stitch. Snip loose ends.

When the stitches of the long-stem fly stitch are embroidered end to end, they create a fun bird-track stitch.

The long-stem fly stitch was used to create the nose for the Woolly Sheep pattern.

STEM STITCH

The stem stitch creates a decorative rope-like line that can be embroidered on top of wool felt and other appliqué patterns. The thicker the yarn or floss used, the thicker the line created.

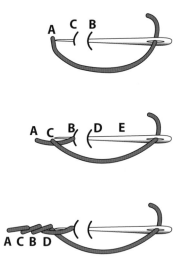

Come up from the bottom of your work at A. Direct the chenille needle from B to C. Moving to the right, continue embroidering from D to B, E to D, and so on. Always keep the floss to one side of the needle and the needle pointed back toward the previous stitch. Make the stitches as even and consistent in size as possible.

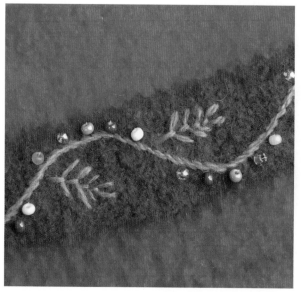

Use the stem stitch to create winding vines, as shown here, simple veins for leaves, and to decoratively outline shapes.

STRAIGHT STITCH

The straight, or running, stitch is the most basic stitch used for topstitching and hand sewing. The key is to keep the stitch length consistent, which requires practice. You can vary the stitch length (on purpose!) to achieve different effects and create interest.

Come up from the bottom of your work at A. Direct the chenille needle back down through the wool at B, making a stitch in a desired length. Repeat as needed. This creates an evenly spaced running line.

Another use for the straight stitch is to embroider random lines to create a larger motif like a holly leaf sprig on the brim of the snowman's black top hat. Use green yarn or floss for the leaf sprigs and red for the French knot berries.

Button It Up: Adding Detail and Whimsy with Buttons

Buttons add unique charm and personality to a felted piece and can have sentimental value, especially if they are from Grandma's old stash. Use different sized buttons to create the effect of polka dots. Layering buttons (smaller buttons on top of larger ones) will create two-toned dots. Flower or snowflake buttons give a spring or wintery theme to a project.

The tools needed are embroidery floss or fingering weight yarn in colors that match the wool background and a needle small enough to fit through the holes of the buttons. Buttons of all sizes, shapes, and colors can be used.

To sew on the buttons, thread the needle with the yarn or floss. Direct the needle up through the bottom of your work. Where the thread emerges, sew a tiny stitch to anchor the thread to the wool. Secure the button to the wool by sewing through the buttonholes at least two to three times.

If the next button will be sewn on within 1 to 2 inches of the last button, direct the needle through the wool to the new button's position. If the next button is to be farther away than this, either cut the thread and begin again or direct the needle through the wool about an inch or so, come up, and immediately go back down, catching a tiny bit of wool as you do, just enough so the thread will not be too noticeable. Then direct the needle through the wool again to the next position. Continue this several times if needed until you reach the new desired button position. This prevents the wool from puckering. When all the buttons are attached, sew a tiny stitch underneath the last button to anchor the thread. Snip the loose ends.

Button Flowers

You can use buttons in several ways to create a floral effect. First, you can sew tiny buttons along an embroidered feather stitch vine, varying their positions. Tiny buttons work best along a vine, but don't be afraid to experiment!

To make button flowers using wool or acrylic felt, cut out felt circles using any size coin as a template. Thread a needle with a brightly colored embroidery floss (all six plies). Direct the needle through the wool about 2 inches/5 cm away from where you will place your first button flower, coming out in the desired position. Anchor the thread by sewing a tiny stitch where the thread emerges.

Direct the needle into the center of one of the felt circles and up through the hole of a small button. This button becomes the flower's center, so choose one small

Buttons can stand alone as a simple flower head or be used as the center of a felt flower.

Here are three different ways to make button flowers—experiment with your own ideas!

enough to fit within the felt circle and that will complement the color of the flower's petals. Direct the needle back down through the other buttonhole, through the felt and into the wool underneath. Sew through the buttonholes two or three times to secure the button, felt, and wool underneath, then direct the needle through the wool to the next intended flower position. If the new button flower will be placed within 1 to 2 inches/2.5 to 5 cm from the last one, direct the needle through the wool to the new flower's position. If it is to be farther away, direct the needle through the wool about an inch or so, come up and immediately go back down, catching a tiny bit of wool as you do, just enough so the thread will not be too noticeable. Then direct the needle through the wool again to the next position. Continue in this way if needed until you reach the new desired position. This prevents the wool from puckering. Pull the thread so the button lays taut against the felt surface. To finish, sew a tiny stitch under the last flower to anchor thread. Snip loose ends.

To create the petals on each flower, cut five to six slits evenly around the felt up to the button's rim. Cut five to six new slits close to the last slits. Pull out and remove the felt between the two slits. If desired, cut the felt with a pair of scissors to round out each petal. The button holds the felt flower in place with no need to tack it down. The felt will not unravel or fray.

Sparkle and Shine: Beads and Sequins

Beads and sequins add small bits of shine, color, and texture to your felted project. Beads and sequins are usually the final touch to any embellishing project. All the materials for beading can be found in a bead or craft store.

Beads: Beads come in glossy or matte finishes. A bead needs to be big enough to not disappear in the wool's thick texture. The two bead sizes recommended for the projects in this book are sizes 8 and 11. The size 11 seed beads are half the size of the size 8 and are used for tiny color accents.

> **Do It Your Way:** Wherever you see size 8 seed beads called for in my projects, you can substitute a French knot, if you prefer. French knots are typically larger than size 8 beads, but they will deliver the same amount of color and texture.

Sequins: Sequins add a lovely sheen and soft, translucent hint of color. They require beads or French knots to anchor them in place on the wool underneath. Create sparkly flowers, shimmery dots, or calico-like textures on your wool project by coupling beads with sequins. Choose beads that will complement the sequin both in size and color. Choose a bead size that will fit within the sequin's shape and size and not overpower it. Size 11 seed beads are a great size to use when beading with sequins. When choosing color combinations, select a bead that will blend with the sequin, but not so much that it will

White or cream size 8 seed beads quickly create tiny polka dots that stand out against the green background of any woolly holiday ornament or egg.

disappear or be overshadowed by it. If the sequin is a pale color, then select a bead color two or three shades darker. On darker sequins, choose contrasting colored beads to stand out boldly against the sequin.

Sequins come in a variety of colors and shapes: circles, squares, flowers, triangles, and stars. Bead stores offer more sequin choices in smaller packages than craft stores. Sequins come and go depending on the latest beading trends, unfortunately. A small package of sequins will embellish several projects, so a little goes a long way!

Thread: The color of the beading thread should match the color of the wool background, not the bead color. With crystal clear bead thread, there is no need to match the floss color to the background wool because it is transparent. It can be used on any color wool with any color bead. FireLine (it's actually transparent fishing line) is sold in bead stores, sporting goods stores, and online. You will find the price in a sporting goods store is more reasonable, and it's usually sold on larger size spools.

Needle: The beading needle needs to be small enough to fit through a variety of bead/sequin sizes. The John James Straw needle, size 11, is small and sturdy enough for beading on wool.

ATTACHING A BEAD

Thread a beading needle with a length of bead thread. Tie a knot at one end. Direct the needle into the wool, coming out where you want to begin beading. Pull the thread until the knot snugs into the wool and doesn't rest on top of it. Sew two to three tiny stitches where the thread emerges to anchor it. Create enough stitches as needed so that when the thread is tugged, it holds its position and doesn't pull out. Insert the needle through the bead and back into the wool at the same spot where the thread emerged. Pull the thread through until the first bead lies taut against the wool surface. The bead should lie flat against the wool, not indented. Direct the needle through the wool to the new bead position.

Continue until all the beads are sewn into position. To end, sew two tiny stitches into the wool's surface. Direct the needle through the wool about 2 inches/5 cm away and come back out. Snip the loose ends.

ATTACHING A SEQUIN WITH A BEAD

Thread a beading needle with bead thread and tie a knot at one end. Direct the needle into the wool, coming out where you want to add a sequin. Pull the thread until the knot snugs into the wool. Sew two to three tiny stitches where the thread emerges to anchor it.

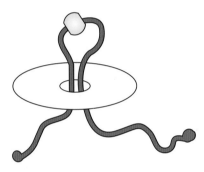

Insert the needle through the hole of the sequin and then up through the hole of the bead. Direct the needle to the top hole of the sequin, bypassing the bead, and back into the wool underneath, at the same spot where the thread emerged. Pull the thread until the sequin lies flat against the wool; it should not indent the wool. The bead acts as a decorative anchor for the sequin, holding the sequin in position. Direct the needle through the wool to the new sequin/bead position.

Continue sewing on beads and sequins until they are all in their desired positions. To end, sew two tiny stitches into the surface of the wool. Direct the needle through the wool about 2 inches/5 cm away and come back out. Snip the thread close to the wool's edge.

Grade-A
Eggs

Knit up a dozen eggs in your choice of sizes (medium and large) just in time for spring! No dyes. No mess. It's an easy pattern that inspires creativity.

Felted Measurements

Medium egg: 3 inches/8 cm long
Large egg: 4 inches/10 cm long

Materials

NOTE: When choosing yarns, do not use a machine washable yarn (like superwash merino), as it will not felt. Also, white yarns generally don't felt well. For a list of cream and other off-white yarns that do felt reliably, see page 2.

Medium Egg
- 17 yd./16 m 100% wool #2 sport weight or #3 light worsted weight yarn
- US 8/5 mm set of double-pointed needles

Large Egg
- 20 yd./18.5 m 100% wool #4 medium worsted weight yarn
- US 10½/6.5 mm set of double-pointed needles

Both Sizes
- Split ring stitch marker
- Scissors
- Tapestry needle
- Chenille needle
- Polyester fiberfill or wool stuffing

Special Stitches

inc 1: Increase one stitch by knitting into the front and then back of same stitch.

ssk: Slip, slip, knit. Slip one stitch as if to knit onto the right needle, then slip another in the same way. Insert the left needle into the front of the two slipped stitches. Knit these stitches together; this creates a left-slanting decrease.

Small egg cartons make wonderful display holders for the medium-size eggs.

On preceding page: *These medium-size eggs were all knit using Cascade 220 sport weight yarns.*

Grade-A Eggs

With #2 sport weight or #3 light worsted weight yarn and US 8/5 mm dpns (for a medium-size egg) or #4 medium worsted weight yarn and US 10$\frac{1}{2}$/6.5 mm dpns (for a large egg), CO 8 sts.

Row 1: *Inc 1, k1*; repeat *to* to end of rnd (12 sts). Divide sts evenly between 3 dpns, taking care not to twist them.

Rnd 2: Join to work in the rnd, knit. Place stitch marker to indicate beg of rnd.

Rnd 3: Knit.

Rnd 4: *Inc 1, k1*; repeat *to* to end of rnd (18 sts).

Rnd 5: Knit.

Rnd 6: *Inc 1, k2*; repeat *to* to end of rnd (24 sts).

Rnd 7: Knit.

Rnd 8: *Inc 1, k3*; repeat *to* to end of rnd (30 sts).

Rnds 9–18: Knit.

Rnd 19: *K3, ssk*; repeat *to* to end of rnd (24 sts).

Rnd 20: Knit.

Rnd 21: *K2, k2tog*; repeat *to* to end of rnd (18 sts).

Rnd 22: Knit.

Rnd 23: *K1, ssk*; repeat *to* to end of rnd (12 sts).

Rnd 24: Knit.

Rnd 25: *K2tog*; repeat *to* to end of rnd (6 sts).

Break yarn, leaving a 6-inch/15 cm tail. Using a tapestry needle, thread tail through remaining 6 sts and tie off, securing the end. Secure all loose ends. Leave the opening at the bottom of the egg unsewn. Once felted, this opening will allow ample room to stuff the egg with fiberfill.

Felting the Eggs

Machine felt the eggs as directed on pages 4–7 until the knit stitches are no longer recognizable and the wet eggs when laid out flat measure about 3$\frac{1}{2}$ inches/9 cm long for the medium-size egg and 4$\frac{1}{2}$ inches/12.5 cm for the large.

While felting, keep an eye out: The opening of the egg can felt shut, especially on the medium size. As it felts, occasionally poke your finger into the opening as needed to enlarge it slightly. Once fully felted, remove the egg from the washing machine and rinse in cold water to get the soap out. Gently wring as much water out as you can without distorting the shape, and then blot the egg dry between towels. Tug and pull the egg into the desired oval shape.

Stuffing the Eggs

While the eggs are still wet, stuff them as full as you can with either polyester or wool fiberfill. If the egg's hole sealed during felting, snip a tiny slit in one end wide enough to get the stuffing in. Once stuffed and still wet, take a strand of matching yarn and with a chenille needle sew the opening closed. You will find the wet wool to be more pliable for stitching less visible seams. Allow the egg to air dry completely.

Getting It Just Right

If your stuffed egg looks lopsided or lumpy, thoroughly wet it, and then squeeze out the excess water. Reshape the egg between the palms of your hands, molding it to perfection. Allow it to air dry completely. This rewetting/reshaping process can be repeated again even after embellishing.

Medium-size eggs fit comfortably within decorative eggcups. A whimsical display for those prized embellished eggs!

Making Your Grade-A Eggs "Egg-stra" Special

PRE-FELTING EMBELLISHMENTS

Striped Eggs

For striped eggs, simply change colors while you are knitting. This is a nice way to use up short lengths of yarn you may have in your stash. Just be sure all the yarn you use for any particular egg is all from the same brand to ensure consistent felting.

Always begin a new color at the beginning of a round. One round of color will felt into a thin line; depending on the yarn, it might get lost in the final felted fabric. For a more substantial stripe, knit two or more rounds. The different yarn colors can be loosely carried up the inside of the egg—no need to break the yarn at each color change. Be sure to secure all the loose ends and seal any holes created from the adding of new colors before proceeding to felting.

Experiment with various thicknesses of stripes, incorporating as many coordinating yarn colors as desired.

Speckled Eggs

Knit the Grade-A Eggs pattern with two or more yarns together using $10^{1}/_{2}$/6.5 mm dpns to create speckled eggs! See page 13 for advice on color combinations. The speckled egg will felt bigger than the large-size egg in the end, with the finished size dependent on the number of yarns carried together.

The orange yarn was a worsted yarn and the periwinkle, a sport weight. The thinner yarn weight gives a hint of blue speckling within the egg after felting.

Beribboned Eggs

For this, you will work a series of yarn overs around the middle of the knitted egg. Once felted, a ribbon will be woven through the holes and tied into a bow. Choose a ribbon color that complements the egg yarns and any embroidery stitches.

Wire ribbon holds its shape the best, long after that initial bow is tied!

Follow the instructions for the Grade-A Eggs pattern until Rnd 16.

Rnd 16: K3, [yo, k2tog, yo, k2tog, k3] 3 times, yo, k2tog, yo, k2tog, k2 (30 sts).

There should be eight holes total. Finish the egg pattern according to the Grade-A Egg pattern instructions. Before felting, lace a shoestring through the holes and loosely tie the ends together. The shoestring will keep the holes from closing during felting.

Once the egg is felted, stuff it and sew the bottom opening closed. Pull out the shoestring and cut an 18-inch/46 cm length of ribbon that is $3/4$ to $1^1/2$ inches/2 to 5 cm wide. Wire ribbon holds its shape the best over time. Thread a tapestry needle with the ribbon, folding the ribbon if needed to fit within the eye of the needle. Starting with any hole, weave the needle in the hole and immediately out of the next. Direct the ribbon to the next pair of holes and continue weaving in this manner (four times total). Adjust the ribbon so the ends are equal in length and tie them into a bow. Shape the bow and trim away any excess.

POST-FELTING EMBELLISHMENTS

For the techniques used to create the suggested effects below, see For the Love of Detail chapter for further information.

Polka-Dot Eggs

This can be done in several ways. Tiny dots can be added using colorful beads. Small dots can be needle felted on using small pinches of roving. Larger polka dots can be cut from acrylic or wool felt and needle felted or embroidered onto the egg. Create a coordinated series of eggs that can be displayed in a decorative bowl or basket.

These five eggs create a series, each knit in different combinations of four yarn colors. After being felted, these same yarns were used to further embellish the eggs with embroidered stitches, polka dots, and squiggles.

Buttoned-Up Eggs

Using round buttons creates another kind of polka dot. Layering buttons, one on top of the other, adds texture and dimension to an egg. Seasonally themed buttons such as pumpkins or gingerbread men coordinate with a holiday theme.

Different size buttons with two or four holes in the same color scheme create whimsical polka dots. When sewing on a white button, use floss in a color that contrasts with the wool underneath to add a little color.

Appliqué Eggs

Any kind of shape can be cut from acrylic or wool felt and appliquéd to the egg using the blanket or overhand embroidery stitch. Cotton floss or two-ply wool yarns and a chenille needle can be used for embroidering along the edge of the felt cutout.

After the appliqué flower and leaf were embroidered into place, a stem stitch vine was added. Sprinkled into the mix are a few green seed beads.

Bead-Spangled Eggs

Beads and sequins will add sparkle and shine to your woolly eggs. They can be worked as part of a larger needle-felted design or as simple accents to embroidery—whatever suits your fancy.

Beads and sequins are an easy way to create a variety of polka dots in different sizes. The feather stitch was embroidered using all six plies of a yellow floss. The sheen of the cotton floss complements the sparkle of the beads.

Freestyling Eggs

Vines and curls can be added to any egg using needle felting. Fingering weight yarns create thin line-like vines, while bulkier yarns create more substantial lines. All sorts of designs can be added by needle felting wool roving, yarn scraps, and felt pieces to an egg.

The flower was needle felted to the egg using layers of pink and orange wool roving. The leaves were cut from wool felt and then needle felted onto the egg. The blanket stitch and French knots were embroidered around the flower, creating additional color accents and texture.

Embroidered Eggs

Embroidery stitches add whimsy to any egg, whether to enhance a knitted stripe or separate two areas of color. Use a variety of colored flosses, even variegated ones, to add more colors to the scheme.

Variegated cotton sport weight yarn was used to embroider the feather stitch around this egg. The variegated yarn complements the felted egg colors.

Woolly Sheep

These folk art-like sheep are fun to knit up and felt. Create your own unique flock: a woolly sheep that has a fuzzy boiled-wool texture, a curly-haired sheep made with curly mohair locks, and a sheep knitted using a large loopy stitch that felts into a bumpy, nubby texture.

Felted Measurements

About 4¹/₂ to 5 inches/11.5 to 12.5 cm wide by 6 inches/15.25 cm high with legs and after being stuffed with fiberfill

Materials

NOTE: When choosing yarns, do not use a machine washable yarn (like superwash merino) as it will not felt. Also, white yarns generally don't felt well. For a list of cream and other off-white yarns that do felt reliably, see page 2. The colors and brands listed are for the sheep in the photo opposite.

- Color A (body): 49 yd./45 m 100% wool cream #4 worsted weight yarn (shown opposite using Cascade 220 Worsted #8010 Cream, 220 yd./200 m per skein)
- Color B (head, ears, and legs): 16 yd./15 m black 100% wool #4 worsted weight yarn (shown opposite using Cascade 220 Worsted #8555 Black, 220 yd./200 m per skein)
- US size 10¹/₂/6.5 mm set of double-pointed needles
- US size 10¹/₂/6.5 mm circular needles, 16 inches/41 cm long
- Split ring stitch markers
- Tapestry needle
- Polyester fiberfill stuffing
- Small cowbell or jingle bell
- Twine or string, for tying on bell
- 2 pieces of ¹/₈-inch/.3-cm-wide grosgrain ribbon, each 25 inches/63.5 cm long, for felting the legs
- Two 8-inch/20 cm lengths black 18-gauge craft wire, for legs
- Gray or pink #1 fingering weight yarn or embroidery floss, for nose
- Chenille needle

Special Stitches

inc 1: Increase one stitch by knitting into the front and then back of same stitch.

ssk: Slip, slip, knit. Slip one stitch as if to knit onto the right needle, then slip another in the same way. Insert the left needle into the front of the two slipped stitches. Knit these stitches together; this creates a left-slanting decrease.

Woolly Sheep

SHEEP'S BODY

Using Color A yarn and dpns, CO 12 sts. Divide sts evenly among 3 dpns, taking care not to twist them. Join to work in the rnd.

Rnd 1: *Inc 1, k1*; repeat *to* to end of rnd (18 sts). Place a stitch marker to indicate beg of rnd.

Rnd 2: Knit.

Rnd 3: *Inc 1, k2*; repeat *to* to end of rnd (24 sts).

Rnd 4: Knit.

Rnd 5: *Inc 1, k3*; repeat *to* to end of rnd (30 sts).

Rnd 6: Knit.

NOTE: In Rnd 7, openings will be created for the sheep's legs. Cut four 10-inch/25 cm lengths of scrap yarn.

***On preceding page:** Knit your very own flock of sheep. Be sure to include a black sheep—every family has one!*

Rnd 7:

(Leg 1): K1, drop sheep yarn, join one piece of scrap yarn, knit 2 sts, drop scrap yarn, leaving the ends hanging. Slide these 2 sts back onto left needle. Pick up the sheep yarn and knit 11 sts.

(Leg 2): Drop sheep yarn, join second piece of scrap yarn, knit 2 sts, and drop scrap yarn. Slide these 2 sts back onto left needle. Pick up the sheep yarn and knit 4 sts.

(Leg 3): Drop sheep yarn, join third piece of scrap yarn, knit 2 sts, and drop scrap yarn. Slide these 2 sts back onto left needle. Pick up the sheep yarn and knit 11 sts.

(Leg 4): Drop sheep yarn, join fourth piece of scrap yarn, knit 2 sts, and drop scrap yarn. Slide these 2 sts back onto left needle. Pick up the sheep yarn and knit 3 sts to end of rnd.

Rnd 8: Knit.

Rnd 9: *K2, inc 1, k9, inc 1, k2*; repeat *to* to end of rnd (34 sts).

Rnd 10: Knit.

Rnd 11: *K2, inc 1, k11, inc 1, k2*; repeat *to* to end of rnd (38 sts).

Rnd 12: Change to circular needles, knit.

Rnd 13: *K2, inc 1, k13, inc 1, k2*; repeat *to* to end of rnd (42 sts).

Rnd 14: Knit.

Rnd 15: *K2, inc 1, k15, inc 1, k2*; repeat *to* to end of rnd (46 sts).

Rnds 16–30: Knit.

NOTE: In Rnd 31 an opening will be created for the sheep's head. Cut one 15-inch/38 cm piece of scrap yarn.

Rnd 31: P2, k24, drop sheep yarn, join scrap yarn, knit 6 sts, and drop scrap yarn, leaving ends hanging. Slide these 6 sts back onto left needle. Pick up the sheep yarn and knit to last 2 sts, p2. The purl stitches will be picked up later for the tail.

Rnd 32: Knit.

Rnd 33: K2, ssk, k21, k2tog, k4, ssk, k9, k2tog, k2 (42 sts).

Rnd 34: Knit 21 sts onto one dpn, knit rem 21 sts onto a second dpn. Transfer the stitch marker. This marker stays in place until the pattern is completed.

Keeping the stitches on both needles, carefully turn the work inside out so the purl side is now facing out. With the needles parallel to each other, do a three-needle bind-off, as follows: Insert another dpn kwise into the first stitch on both needles. Knit them together as one stitch. Repeat so two stitches are now on the right needle. Loosely BO by passing the right stitch over the left and off the needle. One stitch will be left on the right needle. Repeat to end. Break Color A yarn and tie off. Turn the work inside out so the knit side is now facing out.

SHEEP'S HEAD

NOTE: If you prefer an all-cream sheep, substitute cream yarn for the black.

Carefully pull out the scrap yarn you knit in for the sheep's head in Rnd 31, stitch by stitch, creating 12 live stitches. Divide these evenly between two dpns. With the bind-off seam facing you, join Color B yarn.

Rnd 1: Knit across 6 sts and pick up and knit 1 st in the space after the sixth st. Knit across the second needle and pick up and knit 1 st before the beg of the rnd for a total of 14 sts, with 7 sts on each dpn. Place a stitch marker to indicate beg of rnd. This marker will be used later for placement of the ears.

Rnd 2: Knit.

Rnd 3: P2, k3, p2, k7. The purl stitches will be picked up later for the ears.

Rnds 4–8: Knit.

Rnd 9: *K2tog*; repeat *to* to end of rnd (7 sts).

Rnd 10: Knit.

Break Color B, leaving a 6-inch/15-cm tail. Using a tapestry needle, thread the tail through the remaining 7 sts and tie off. Secure all loose ends.

SHEEP'S EARS

NOTE: If you prefer an all-cream sheep, substitute cream yarn for the black.

Right Ear

Position the sheep's head so the stitch marker is on the right. Use a dpn to pick up the 2 top purl loops on the right side of the head. Do not turn work. Slide sts to the right of the needle.

Row 1: Join Color B, inc 1, k1 (3 sts).

Row 2: Purl.

Row 3: Knit.

Rows 4–5: Rep Rows 2–3.

Row 6: P3tog (1 st).

Break Color B, leaving a 6-inch/15-cm tail and tie off.

Left Ear

Position the sheep's head so the first ear is on the right. With a dpn, pick up the 2 top purl loops on the left side. Do not turn work. Slide sts to the right of the needle.

Row 1: Join Color B, k1, inc 1 (3 sts).

Row 2: Purl.

Row 3: Knit.

Rows 4–5: Rep Rows 2–3.

Row 6: P3tog (1 st).

Break Color B, leaving a 6-inch/15-cm tail and tie off. Secure all loose ends.

SHEEP'S TAIL

Remove the stitch marker at the sheep's back end. With the sheep's head facing away from you, pick up the 4 top purl loops near the top of the sheep. Do not turn work. Slide sts to the right of the needle.

Row 1: Join Color A, purl to end.

Row 2: Knit.

Row 3: Purl.

Row 4: Ssk, k2tog (2 sts).

Row 5: P2tog (1 st).

Break Color A, leaving a 6-inch/15-cm tail and tie off. Secure all loose ends.

SHEEP'S LEGS

NOTE: If you prefer an all-cream sheep, substitute cream yarn for the black.

Pull out one of the four scrap yarns from Rnd 7, stitch by stitch, creating 4 live stitches. Divide these stitches evenly between two dpns.

Rnd 1: Join Color B, knit 2 sts, then pick up and knit 1 st in the space after the second st. Knit across the second needle and pick up and knit 1 st before beg of the rnd for a total of 6 sts, with 3 sts on each of two dpns. Insert one length of grosgrain ribbon up through the bottom center hole of the sheep and through this leg hole.

Rnd 2: *K1, k2tog*; repeat *to* to end of rnd and all sts are on one dpn (4 sts). Do not turn work. Slide sts to the right of the needle.

Rnd 3: Keeping the ribbon in the center, pull the yarn from the back of the work over the ribbon, and knit. Do not turn work. Slide sts to the right of the needle.

Rnds 4–8: Rep Rnd 3, keeping the ribbon running up the center of the leg.

Break Color B, leaving a 6-inch/15-cm tail. With a tapestry needle, thread the tail through the remaining 4 sts from right to left (encircling the ribbon) and tie off. Repeat this process for the other legs. Use one length of ribbon for the front legs and a second length for the back. Secure all loose ends.

Securely tie the ribbon ends together (front to front and back to back) to keep them from coming undone while felting. The legs will shrink, but the ribbon will prevent them from sealing shut so the wire can later be inserted. Leave the opening at the bottom of the sheep unsewn. This opening will allow access to stuff the body with fiberfill after felting.

Felting the Sheep

Machine felt the sheep as directed on pages 4–7 according to color: light sheep with light, dark sheep with dark. A bicolored sheep (cream body with black face) can be felted in a light color load. The sheep will felt within two to four cycles. While felting, periodically check on the progress of your sheep by pulling them out of the mesh bag. Adjust or retie the leg ribbons if needed. Poke your finger into the sheep's head to make sure it isn't felting shut. This opening will allow access to stuff the head with fiberfill after felting.

Felt your sheep until the knit stitches disappear and the wet sheep laid out flat measures about $4^{1}/_{2}$ to 5 inches/11.5 to 13.75 cm wide and about $4^{1}/_{2}$ inches/11.5 cm high, not including the head and legs. It is important to felt the sheep to these measurements; otherwise, the leg wires will either be too short or too long. Tug and pull the sheep into the desired shape.

Assembling the Sheep

Once completely felted and while still wet, firmly stuff the head with fiberfill. Firmly stuff the sheep's body, rounding out its overall shape. Stretch the ears widthwise to create a full oval disk. If needed, trim the ears to round out their ends. Using T-pins, pin the tail and the ears into their desired positions. Pin the head down close to the body. Pull the ribbons out of the legs.

FINISHING THE LEGS

While the sheep is still wet, take one of the 8-inch/20-cm lengths of black craft wire, measure $1^{1}/_{2}$ inches/4 cm from one end, and bend it over on itself at that point. Twist the folded end over onto itself as shown in Diagram 1. Now measure $1^{1}/_{2}$ inches/4 cm from the other end, bend it over on itself at that point, and then twist the folded end over onto itself as you did for the other side. With a wire cutter trim any sharp edges. Repeat with the second length of wire.

Thread one wire through the bottom center hole of the sheep and up the whole length of one of the felted legs. If the wire's folded loop is too wide to fit within the leg, slightly squeeze the loop with needle-nose pliers. Kitty-corner from the first leg, thread the other folded

Stuff the head until firm but not too big, tapering it back from the nose to the body. After the body has dried, the head can be needle felted into perfection, slightly smaller and tapered, if desired.

loop up through the inside of this leg. Repeat with the second folded wire and remaining two legs. The two wires should crisscross each other inside the sheep.

Using black yarn and a chenille needle, sew a few stitches through the wire loops to secure to the wool and close the holes left by the ribbons. If creating an all-cream sheep, use appropriate leg yarn color. Stand the sheep up and allow it to air dry completely in this position.

1¹/₂"

Diagram 1

SEWING UP THE SHEEP

Once the sheep is dried, close the opening at the bottom of the sheep. Thread the chenille needle with a strand of sheep yarn, knotting one end. Sew a running stitch along the outside edge of the opening as shown in Diagram 2.

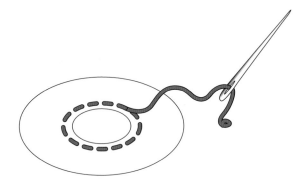

Diagram 2

Gently pull the attached yarn until the opening cinches shut as tightly as possible. Sew at least five tiny stitches to seal the hole completely. Bury the loose end within the sheep.

ADDING THE SHEEP'S NOSE

To embroider the nose, thread the chenille needle with a strand of gray or pink fingering weight yarn or embroidery floss (all six plies). Begin embroidering the long-stem fly stitch as shown in Diagram 3 (for instructions on how to make this stitch, see page 23). To finish, direct the needle back into the sheep's head and out the back. Snip all loose ends.

Diagram 3

BRUSHING THE SHEEP'S FLEECE

If alpaca or mohair yarn was used to create the sheep, then vigorously brushing the felted wool will create a soft and fluffy sheep. A great tool for brushing wool is a nap riser, a small, fine, soft-wire brush that is held on two fingers. The wire bristles pull at the yarn, causing the fine hairs to spring out of the felted wool. Vigorously brush one way and then back the other. A small dog brush also works well.

ADDING THE DECORATIVE BELL

Cut a 10-inch/25-cm length of twine or string. Slip the bell onto the twine and loosely tie it around the sheep's neck. Trim the ends.

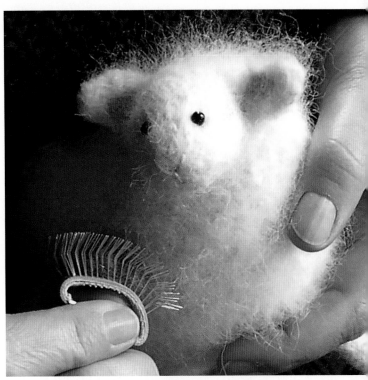

An optional idea is to add pink accents to your all-cream sheep's ears using little bits of pale pink roving and needle felting. Poke the roving into the ears at an angle, otherwise the pink roving will show up on the ear's back side.

Optional eyes can be added to your little lamb by sewing on glossy black seed beads using white bead thread.

Curly Locks Sheep

C over your felted sheep with a luxurious coat of soft and silky mohair! This curly coat is quick and easy with whimsical results!

Materials

- 1 felted and finished all-cream (body, head, legs) Woolly Sheep; you'll need 65 yd./60 m 100% wool cream #4 worsted weight yarn for this
- One 1-ounce/.04-g bag of natural cream-colored curly mohair locks (look for these online or at local sheep and wool festivals)
- 38-gauge all-purpose felting needle
- Pink embroidery floss, for nose

Assembling the Curly Locks Sheep

Once your Woolly Sheep is felted and finished, you can start attaching the curly locks. Pull a small clump of locks from the package. Using the felting needle, begin poking the locks onto the sheep's body, basting each clump in place. Pull off another clump and repeat the process until the body is covered, but not the head and legs.

Go back now and needle felt the locks gently to secure them from being tugged loose, but try not to flatten or crush the locks, keeping the curls intact. The locks can be fluffed by gently rubbing them with your fingers.

A simple nose is created using pink DMC embroidery floss, all six plies, and embroidering a long-stemmed fly stitch.

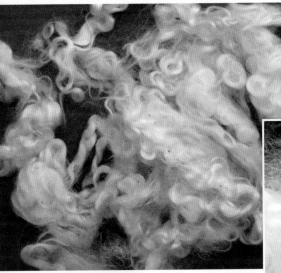

A one-ounce package of natural cream-colored mohair curls.

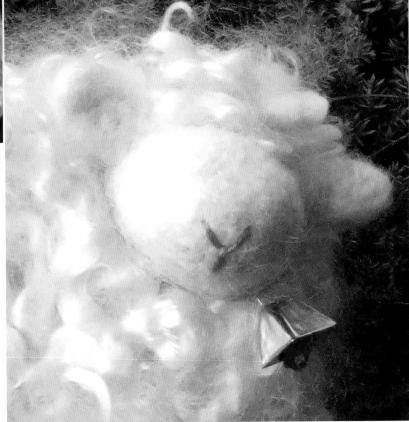

On preceding page: *Needle felt mohair locks onto your Woolly Sheep for this super curly look!*

Loopy Stitch Sheep

This whimsical addition to the flock is created using the loopy stitch, which felts into a nubby-like texture, fun to cuddle and touch!

Materials

Same as for Woolly Sheep (page 35), but you will need more of Color A because of the Loopy Stitch: 79 yd./72 m 100% wool cream #4 worsted weight yarn

Loopy Stitch Sheep

SHEEP'S BODY

With Color A yarn and dpns, CO 12 sts. Divide sts evenly among 3 dpns, taking care not to twist them. Join to work in the rnd.

Rnd 1: *Inc 1, k1*; repeat *to* to end of rnd (18 sts). Place a stitch marker to indicate beg of rnd.

Rnd 2: Knit.

Rnd 3: *Inc 1, k2*; repeat *to* to end of rnd (24 sts).
Rnd 4: Knit.
Rnd 5: *Inc 1, k3*; repeat *to* to end of rnd (30 sts).
Rnd 6: Knit.
NOTE: In Rnd 7, openings will be created for the sheep's legs. Cut four 10-inch/25-cm lengths of scrap yarn.
Rnd 7:
(Leg 1): K1, drop sheep yarn, join one piece of scrap yarn, knit 2 sts, drop scrap yarn, leaving the ends hanging. Slide these 2 sts back onto left needle. Pick up the sheep yarn and knit 11 sts.
(Leg 2): Drop sheep yarn, join second piece of scrap yarn, knit 2 sts, and drop scrap yarn. Slide these 2 sts back onto left needle. Pick up the sheep yarn and knit 4 sts.

(continued)

Loopy Stitch Sheep before felting.

On preceding page: *This Loopy Stitch Sheep was knit using Patons Classic Wool Worsted #202 Aran and #226 Black.*

Loopy Stitch (LS)

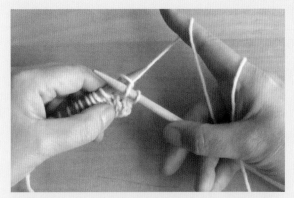

1. Knit into front of stitch but don't take it off needle.

4. Knit into back of stitch.

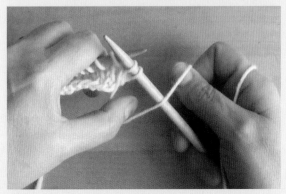

2. Bring yarn to front (between needles) and wrap it around your left thumb.

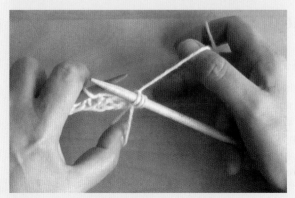

5. Slide this stitch off needle.

3. Move yarn to back (between needles).

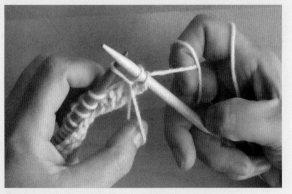

6. On right needle, slip first stitch over second.

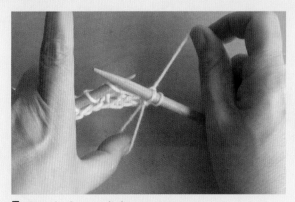

7. Give the loop a slight tug to secure.

(Leg 3): Drop sheep yarn, join third piece of scrap yarn, knit 2 sts, and drop scrap yarn. Slide these 2 sts back onto left needle. Pick up the sheep yarn and knit 11 sts.

(Leg 4): Drop sheep yarn, join fourth piece of scrap yarn, knit 2 sts, and drop scrap yarn. Slide these 2 sts back onto left needle. Pick up the sheep yarn and knit 3 sts to end of rnd.

Rnd 8: Knit.

NOTE: In Rnd 9 the Loopy Stitch (LS) pattern begins.

Rnd 9: *LS, k1*; repeat *to* to end of rnd.

Rnd 10: *K2, inc 1, k9, inc 1, k2*; repeat *to* to end of rnd (34 sts).

NOTE: Adjust the Loopy Stitch pattern around the increase and decrease rnds, because this will throw your count off by one each time you increase or decrease. If the pattern doesn't work out perfectly each time, that's okay. Just knit the Loopy Stitch pattern (LS, k1) as evenly as possible throughout. When in doubt, make a Loopy Stitch!

Rnd 11: K1, *LS, k1*; repeat *to* to end of rnd.

Rnd 12: *K2, inc 1, k11, inc 1, k2*; repeat *to* to end of rnd (38 sts).

Rnd 13: Change to circular needles. *LS, k1*; repeat *to* to end of rnd.

Rnd 14: *K2, inc 1, k13, inc 1, k2*; repeat *to* to end of rnd (42 sts).

Rnd 15: K1, *LS, k1*; repeat *to* to end of rnd.

Rnd 16: *K2, inc 1, k15, inc 1, k2*; repeat *to* to end of rnd (46 sts).

Rnd 17: *LS, k1*; repeat *to* to end of rnd.

Rnd 18: Knit.

Rnd 19: K1, *LS, k1*; repeat *to* to end of rnd.

Rnd 20: Knit.

Rnds 21–28: [Rep Rnds 17–20] 2 times.

Rnd 29: *LS, k1*; repeat *to* to end of rnd.

Rnd 30: Knit.

Rnd 31: K1, *LS, k1*; repeat *to* to end of rnd.

NOTE: In Rnd 32 an opening will be created for the sheep's head. Cut one 15-inch/38-cm piece of scrap yarn.

Rnd 32: K26, drop sheep yarn. Join scrap yarn, knit 6 sts, and drop scrap yarn, leaving ends hanging. Slide these 6 sts back onto left needle. Pick up sheep yarn and knit to end of rnd.

Rnd 33: *LS, k1*; repeat *to* to end of rnd.

Rnd 34: K2, ssk, k21, k2tog, k4, ssk, k9, k2tog, k2 (42 sts).

Rnd 35: K1, *LS, k1* onto two dpns; repeat *to* to end of rnd so there are 21 sts on each dpn. Transfer the stitch marker to indicate beg of rnd.

Keeping sts on both needles, carefully turn the work inside out so the purl side is facing out. With the needles held parallel to each other, do a three-needle bind-off as follows: Insert another dpn kwise into the first stitch on both needles. Knit them together as one stitch. Repeat so two stitches are now on the right

needle. Loosely BO by passing the right stitch over the left and off the needle. One stitch will be left on the right needle. Repeat to the end. Break Color A yarn and tie off. Turn the work inside out so the knit side is now facing out.

Assembling the Loopy Stitch Sheep

Complete the pattern as for Woolly Sheep (pages 37–39), leaving out the tail. Machine felt and complete the sheep according to the Woolly Sheep pattern instructions.

This Loopy Stitch Sheep was knit using Brown Sheep Company Nature Spun Worsted #601 Pepper. A simple holiday collar was cut from green felt into the shape of two holly leaves and a red jingle bell was attached to look like a cluster of berries. Both were tied around the sheep's neck with twine.

Baby
Chick

Knit and felt a few chicks to tuck inside your springtime baskets. These little chicks knit up in minutes, so plan on hatching at least a dozen!

Felted Measurements

3 to 3 1/2 inches/8 to 9 cm wide and 3 1/2 inches/9 cm tall with legs and stuffed with fiberfill

Materials

NOTE: When choosing yarns, do not use a machine washable yarn (like superwash merino) as it will not felt. Yarns containing alpaca or mohair will create the fuzziest chicks. The colors and brands listed are for the chick shown in the photo opposite.

- Color A (body and wings): 24 yd./22 m yellow 100% wool #2 sport weight yarn (shown using Frog Tree Alpaca Sport, 100% alpaca, #10 Canary Yellow, 130 yd./119 m per skein)
- Color B (beak): 2 yd./2 m orange 100% wool #2 sport weight yarn (shown using Frog Tree Alpaca Sport, 100% alpaca, #15 Mango, 130 yd./119 m per skein)
- 1/2 yd./.5 m black 100% wool #2 sport weight yarn (shown using Frog Tree Alpaca sport, #100 Black), for French knot eyes
- US 8/5 mm set of double-pointed needles
- Split-ring stitch markers
- Scissors
- Chenille needle
- Polyester fiberfill stuffing
- Two 13-inch/33-cm lengths of 24-gauge wire (available in bead stores and online), for legs
- Size 6 seed beads in any color, for legs
- Wire cutter and needle-nose pliers

Optional materials for embellishment
- 18-inch/46-cm length of ribbon, 1/2 to 1 inch/1.25 to 2.5 cm wide, to tie around the chick's neck
- Straw-colored wool roving, for bonnet
- Length of any color DMC embroidery floss, for tie and flowers on bonnet
- Seed beads in any color, for tiny flowers and leaves on bonnet
- 38-gauge all-purpose felting needle, for bonnet
- Foam pad for needle felting, for bonnet

Notes

- One 180 yd./165 m skein of sport weight yarn will make about six chicks.
- The pattern begins with the chick's tail, a short I-cord.

Special Stitches

inc 1: Increase one stitch by knitting into the front and then back of same stitch.

ssk: Slip, slip, knit. Slip one stitch as if to knit onto the right needle, then slip another in the same way. Insert the left needle into the front of the two slipped stitches. Knit these stitches together; this creates a left-slanting decrease.

Baby Chick

CHICK'S TAIL AND BODY

With Color A yarn, CO 6 sts. Do not turn work. Slide work to right end of needle.

Rows 1–2: Knit. Do not turn work. Slide work to right end of needle.

Row 3: *Inc 1*; rep *to* to end of row (12 sts). Divide sts evenly among 3 dpns, being careful not to twist them. Join to work in the rnd.

Rnd 4: Knit. Place marker to indicate beg of rnd.

Rnd 5: *Inc 1*; rep *to* to end of rnd (24 sts).

Rnd 6: Knit.

Rnd 7: *K3, inc 1*; rep *to* to end of rnd (30 sts).

Rnd 8: Knit.

Rnd 9: *K4, inc 1*; rep *to* to end of rnd (36 sts).

Rnd 10: Knit.

Rnd 11: *K5, inc 1*; rep *to* to end of rnd (42 sts).

NOTE: The next 7 rows create the opening for the chick's belly. This opening will later be used to stuff the felted chick with fiberfill. Remember, you are knitting in rows not rounds.

Row 12: Knit, turn work.

Row 13: Purl, turn work.

Row 14: Knit.

Row 15: Purl.

Rows 16–17: Rep Rows 14–15.

Row 18: Knit. Do not turn work. Join to first st of Row 18 to work in the rnd again.

(continued)

Rnd 19: *K5, ssk*; rep *to* to end of rnd (36 sts).
Rnd 20: Knit.
Rnd 21: *K4, k2tog*; rep *to* to end of rnd (30 sts).
Rnd 22: Knit.
Rnd 23: *K3, ssk*; rep *to* to end of rnd (24 sts).
Rnd 24: Knit.
Rnd 25: *K2, k2tog*; rep *to* to end of rnd (18 sts).
Rnd 26: Knit.

CHICK'S HEAD AND BEAK

Rnds 1–7: Knit.
Rnd 8: *K1, ssk*; rep *to* to end of rnd (12 sts).
Rnd 9: Knit.
Rnd 10: *K2tog*; rep *to* to end of rnd (6 sts).
Break Color A yarn, leaving a 6-inch/15-cm tail.
Rnd 11: Join Color B yarn for beak, knit.
Rnd 12: *K2tog*; rep *to* to end of rnd (3 sts).
Rnd 13: Knit all sts onto 1 dpn. Do not turn work. Slide the work to the right of the needle.
Rnd 14: Sl 1, k2tog, psso (1 st).

Using a wire ribbon, tie a simple bow around your chick's neck to give the illusion of a bonnet.

Break Color B yarn, leaving a 6-inch/15-cm tail. Thread tail through the remaining stitch and tie off. Secure all holes and loose ends.

CHICK'S WINGS

With Color A yarn, CO 8 sts.
Rows 1–3: Knit.
Row 4: Loosely BO 2 sts, knit to end (6 sts).
Row 5: Knit.
Row 6: Loosely BO 3 sts, knit to end (3 sts).
Rows 7–10: Knit.
Row 11: Sl 1, k2tog, psso (1 st).
Break Color A yarn, leaving a 6-inch/15-cm tail. Thread the tail through the last stitch and tie off. Secure all loose ends. Repeat for a second wing.

Felting the Chick

The wings need to be hand felted (see page 7) until the knit stitches disappear and each felted wing is about one third to one half of its original size. Hand felting will allow you to control the shrinkage, making sure the pair of wings end up the same size and have the same overall shape. Once felted, rinse the wings in cold water to get the soap out, and then blot them between towels. Tug and pull the wings into shape. Let the wings air dry completely on a wire rack.

The body of the chick can be machine felted (see page 4). Be sure to check on its progress periodically, and insert your thumb into the chick's head to make sure the opening doesn't felt shut. Felting is complete when the knit stitches are no longer recognizable and the chick, when laid out flat, measures 4 to $4^1/_2$ inches/10 to 11.5 cm wide and $2^1/_2$ to 3 inches/6 to 7.5 cm tall. It is important to felt the chick to this size; otherwise, it will be too big for the wire legs and won't be able to stand on its own.

Once felted, pull the chick out of the washing machine and hand rinse in cold water to get the soap out. Wring and blot the chick dry between towels.

Assembling the Chick

Firmly stuff the wet chick with fiberfill. Tug it into shape, especially the tail and beak, as they have a tendency to get crushed during felting. Leave the opening at the bottom of the chick unsewn. Allow the chick to air dry completely on a wire rack.

MAKING THE LEGS

Fold in half one of the lengths of 24-gauge wire. With the two ends facing you, slide eight beads onto the left side of the wire. Slide the first bead (the anchor bead) so it is closer to the fold. Hold the other seven beads between your fingers and thread the end of the right wire through the seven beads. Use the needle-nose pliers to pull the threaded wire until snug around the anchor bead, as shown in Diagram 1.

Diagram 1

Slide another five beads onto the right-side wire of the first beaded toe. Slide the bead nearest the wire's end (anchor bead) slightly to the right. With the end, bypass the anchor bead and thread the wire through the other beads. Hold the other four beads between your fingers and, using the needle-nose pliers, pull the wire away from you until it lies snug around the anchor bead. Two toes are complete.

On the wire left of the first toe, slide on another five beads and repeat the above process for the third toe.

To create the back toe, on the longest wire slide on another four beads. Repeat the above process for the back toe. One webbed foot is complete as shown in Diagram 2.

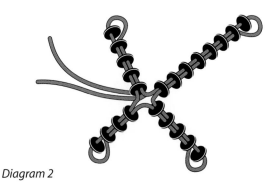

Diagram 2

To finish the leg, thread more beads onto both wire ends for a total of thirteen beads. Firmly push on the first couple of beads to slightly close the gap between all the toes. Set the first leg aside. Repeat the instructions and make a second foot and leg.

The chick's wing is positioned with the longest feather toward the front.

ATTACHING THE LEGS

When both legs are complete, pull all the fiberfill out of the chick's belly. About $1/2$ inch/1.25 cm from one side of the belly opening, poke each leg wire $1/8$ inch/.3 cm apart from each other into the felted wool. Inside the chick, twist the two wires of one leg together against the inside wall. Twist all the way up the wire's length to create one thick wire. Attach the other leg to the other side of the opening in the same way.

Inside the chick, wrap both sets of leg wires around one another, making one continuous wire connecting both legs, like an upside-down U. This is important, otherwise the wires will be too loose, and the chick won't be able to stand on its own. With a wire cutter, trim any sharp ends.

Firmly restuff the chick's body with fiberfill. With a strand of yellow yarn and the chenille needle, sew the opening closed. Secure all loose ends.

The chick is now ready to stand. Keep adjusting the legs and toes slightly to find the right balancing point. If the chick has been felted to the correct size, it will stand on its own!

ATTACHING THE WINGS

With a strand of yellow yarn and the chenille needle, sew the wings onto the chick using the overhand stitch and making very small stitches. Position the wing so the longest feather is toward the front, as shown in the photo above. Stitch along the wing's straight edge.

Making Baby Chick a Bonnet

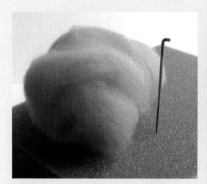

To make the chick's bonnet, you'll need straw-color wool roving, a felting needle, and a foam pad.

1. Pull off a 1- to 2- inch/2.5- to 5-cm pinch of the wool roving.

2. Fold it over onto itself several times.

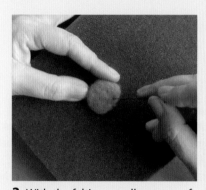

3. With the felting needle on top of the foam pad, begin poking the roving into a 1-inch/2.5-cm round disk. Occasionally rotate the disk, flipping it over so it doesn't end up felted to the pad. Keep poking and shaping the roving until it is fairly flat and rounded.

4. Pull off a smaller piece of roving and gently roll it into a loose ball between your palms.

5. Center this ball on top of the disk (the bonnet's base). Start poking all along the edges of the ball to adhere it to the base, leaving about ¼-inch/.5-cm space all around the ball for the brim of the hat.

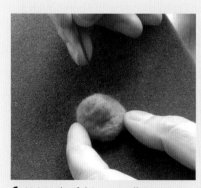

6. Using the felting needle, start rounding the ball into a dome shape, keeping it slightly raised. Continue to flatten and round the brim.

7. Flip the bonnet over and gently poke the center of the underside with the felting needle to create a slight indent for the chick's head.

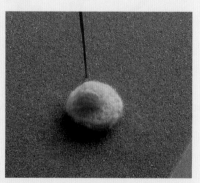

8. The needle-felted bonnet is now ready for a little embellishing!

FINISHING THE CHICK

Using the black yarn and chenille needle, embroider two French knots for the chick's eyes on either side of the beak. Or, if you'd rather, you can sew on glossy black seed beads. (See page 21 or 26 for tutorial.)

If alpaca or mohair yarn was used to create the chick, vigorously brushing the felted wool will create a soft and fluffy chick. A great tool for brushing wool is a nap riser, a small, fine, soft-wire brush that is held on two fingers. The wire bristles pull at the yarn, causing the fine hairs to spring out of the felted wool. Vigorously brush one way and then back the other. A small dog brush also works well.

Tie a length of ribbon around the chick's neck into a small bow. Trim any excess ribbon. To secure the ribbon to the chick's neck, sew a few tiny stitches here and there along the ribbon. Instead of the tied ribbon idea, another option is a sweet and easy needle-felted bonnet for your little chick (see instructions opposite).

EMBELLISHING THE BONNET

Decorate the roving bonnet with little French knots and seed beads. The French knots create small rose-like flowers. Using a chenille needle and brightly colored DMC floss (all six plies), embroider three to five French knots along the front of the brim. Sew tiny green seed beads among the roses to represent the leaves. Add a white or

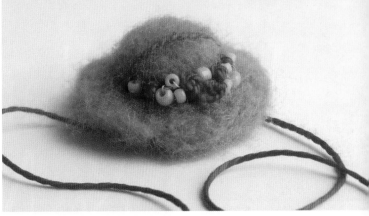

A straw-like bonnet adds the finishing touch to your sweet little chick, adorned in her Sunday best.

orange bead or two for additional color. Cut off and bury the thread ends within the bonnet.

To create a tie for the bonnet, thread the chenille needle with a 12-inch/30.5-cm strand of the same embroidery floss you used to make the French knots. Where the dome of the hat and the brim meet, direct the needle up from the bottom and over the dome and back into the brim on the other side. Adjust the lengths equally by gently pulling the floss so as not to crease or indent the dome. The lengths should be long enough to tie a bow with.

Place the bonnet on the chick's head and loosely tie the strings into a small bow under the chick's chin. Trim any excess ends.

Peep! Peep! Your chick is now fully hatched and ready for the spring parade!

Woodland Gnome
& Mushroom

Knit and felt a whimsical gnome and tuck him in amongst a woodland garden of red mushrooms. According to German folklore, the garden gnome symbolizes good luck. This same gnome pattern is adapted to create Matilda the Witch, Jolly St. Nick, and Lucky the Leprechaun—truly a gnome for all seasons. For whatever the occasion, your little gnome will be ready and willing.

Felted Measurements

Gnome (and his variations—Matilda the Witch, St. Nick, and Leprechaun): 7 inches/18 cm tall when stuffed with fiberfill from its base to the tip of the hat
Mushroom: 4 inches/10 cm tall

Materials

NOTE: When choosing yarns, do not use a machine washable yarn (like superwash merino) as it will not felt. Also, white yarns generally don't felt well. For a list of cream and other off-white yarns that do felt reliably, see page 2. The colors and brands listed are for the gnome and mushroom shown in the photo opposite.

- Color A (coveralls): 16 yd./15 m green 100% wool #4 medium worsted weight yarn (shown using Brown Sheep Company Nature Spun Worsted, #209 Wood Moss, 245 yd./232 m per skein)
- Color B (face): 9 yd./8.5 m cream 100% wool #4 medium worsted weight yarn (shown using Brown Sheep Company Nature Spun Worsted, #N91 Aran, 245 yd./232 m per skein)
- Color C (shoes and hat): 22 yd./20.5 m red #4 medium worsted weight yarn (shown using Brown Sheep Company Nature Spun Worsted, #146 Pomegranate, 245 yd./232 m per skein)
- Color D (mushroom stem): 22 yd./20.5 m cream 100% wool #4 medium worsted weight yarn (shown using Cascade 220 Worsted, #8010 Cream, 220 yd./200 m per skein)
- Color E (mushroom cap): 20 yd./18.5 m red 100% wool #4 medium worsted weight yarn (shown using Cascade 220 Worsted, #8895 Red, 220 yd./200 m per skein)
- US size 10¹/₂/6.5 mm set of double-pointed needles
- US size 10¹/₂/6.5 mm circular needles, any length, used for picking up sts around the hat's brim
- Split-ring stitch marker
- Tapestry needle
- Chenille needle
- Polyester fiberfill
- Plastic poly-pellets
- 1 box Shout® ColorCatcher®, to prevent color bleeding
- 1 or 2 (¹/₂-inch/1.25 cm) button(s)
- Red wool roving, for nose
- White or cream wool roving, for beard
- 38-gauge all-purpose felting needle
- 2 black 4 mm round beads, for eyes
- John James size 11 straw bead needle, for eyes
- White bead thread, for eyes

Notes

- The gnome is knit from the bottom up in the round.
- The brim of his hat is added by picking up stitches around the hat and doing an I-cord bind-off.
- For the gnome's shoes, stitches are picked up and knit.

Special Stitches

inc 1: Increase one stitch by knitting into the front and then back of same stitch.

ssk: Slip, slip, knit. Slip one stitch as if to knit onto the right needle, then slip another in the same way. Insert the left needle into the front of the two slipped stitches. Knit these stitches together; this creates a left-slanting decrease.

Woodland Gnome

GNOME'S COVERALLS

With Color A yarn and dpns, CO 12 sts. Divide the sts evenly among 3 dpns, taking care not to twist them. Join to work in the rnd.

Rnd 1: *Inc , k1*; repeat *to* to end of rnd. Place a stitch marker to indicate beg of rnd (18 sts).

Rnd 2: Knit.

Rnd 3: *Inc 1, k2*; repeat *to* to end of rnd (24 sts).

Rnd 4: Knit.

Rnd 5: *Inc 1, k3*; repeat *to* to end of rnd (30 sts), then turn work.

Rnd 6: Knit.

Rnd 7: Sl 1 st, knit to end of rnd.

Rnd 8: K1, p12, k17. These 12 purl sts will be picked up later for the gnome's two shoes.

Rnds 9–18: Knit.

Break Color A yarn, leaving a 6-inch/15-cm tail.

GNOME'S FACE

Rnd 1: Join Color B yarn, knit.

Rnds 2–7: Knit.

Break Color B yarn, leaving a 6-inch/15-cm tail.

GNOME'S HAT

Rnd 1: Join Color C yarn, knit.

Rnd 2: Purl. These purl sts will be picked up later for the brim of the gnome's hat.

Rnd 3: Knit.

Rnd 4: K2tog, k13, k2tog, k13 (28 sts).

Rnd 5: *K1, ssk, k8, k2tog, k1*; repeat *to* to end of rnd (24 sts).

Rnds 6–8: Knit.

Rnd 9: *K1, ssk, k6, k2tog, k1*; repeat *to* to end of rnd (20 sts).

Rnds 10–12: Knit.

Rnd 13: *K1, ssk, k4, k2tog, k1*; repeat *to* to end of rnd (16 sts).

Rnds 14–16: Knit.

Rnd 17: *K1, ssk, k2, k2tog, k1*; repeat *to* to end of rnd (12 sts).

Rnd 18: K6 sts onto one dpn and 6 onto second dpn.

Rnds 19–20: Knit.

Rnd 21: *K1, ssk, k2tog, k1*; repeat *to* to end of rnd (8 sts).

Rnds 22–24: Knit.

Rnd 25: *K2tog*; repeat *to* until all sts are on one dpn (4 sts). Do not turn work. Slide the work to the right of the needle.

Rnd 26: Knit. Do not turn work. Slide the work to the right of the needle.

Rnds 27–31: Rep Rnd 26.

Break Color C yarn, leaving a 6-inch/15-cm tail. Using a tapestry needle, thread tail through remaining 4 sts and tie off.

BRIM OF GNOME'S HAT

With the circular needle, pick up the bottom loop of each purl st around the base of the hat for a total of 30 sts.

With Color C yarn and dpns, CO 3 sts. Do not turn work. Begin knitting the I-cord bind-off as follows: Slide the 3 sts from the dpn onto the tip of left circular needle. With the dpn, knit the first 2 sts off, and then slip the next st as if to knit. Knit another st from the circular needle and pass the slipped st over the previously knitted st and off the needle. Slide these 3 sts from the dpn back onto the circular needle. Repeat this process until only 3 sts remain on the dpn. Break Color C yarn, leaving a 6-inch/15-cm tail. Using a tapestry needle, thread tail through remaining 3 sts from right to left and tie off. Sew both I-cord ends to the gnome's hat, overlapping them slightly so they appear as one continuous cord.

GNOME'S SHOES

With a dpn and the gnome's bottom facing you, pick up the top loop of each of the 12 purl sts, just up from the base of the gnome. With the bottom of the gnome still facing you, join Color C yarn.

Row 1: P6, then turn work (6 sts).

Row 2: Knit.

Row 3: Purl.

Rows 4–7: [Rep Rows 2–3] 2 times.

NOTE: Be sure the shoes are knit so the knit side is facing upward. Otherwise, the shoes after felting won't curl up.

Row 8: Ssk, k2, k2tog (4 sts).

Row 9: P2tog, p2tog (2 sts).

Row 10: K2tog (1 st).

Break Color C yarn, leaving a 6-inch/15-cm tail, and tie off. This completes one shoe.

With the bottom of the gnome still facing you and the finished shoe on the right, join Color C yarn and repeat Rows 1–10 with the remaining 6 sts for the second shoe. Secure all loose ends.

Woodland Mushroom

MUSHROOM STEM

With Color D yarn and dpns, loosely CO 12 sts. Divide sts evenly between 3 dpns, taking care not to twist them. Join to work in the rnd.

Rnd 1: Knit. Place a stitch marker to indicate beg of rnd.
Rnd 2: Knit.
Rnd 3: *Inc 1, k1*; repeat *to* to end of rnd (18 sts).
Rnd 4: Knit.
Rnd 5: *Inc 1, k2*; repeat *to* to end of rnd (24 sts).
Rnd 6: Knit, then turn work.
Rnd 7: Knit.
Rnd 8: Slip 1 st as if to purl, knit.
Rnds 9–11: Knit.
Rnd 12: *K2, k2tog*; repeat *to* to end of rnd (18 sts).
Rnds 13–17: Knit.
Rnd 18: *K1, ssk*; repeat *to* to end of rnd (12 sts).
Rnds 19–23: Knit.
Break Color D yarn, leaving a 6-inch/15-cm tail.

MUSHROOM CAP

Join Color E yarn.
Rnd 1: *Inc 1, k1*; repeat *to* to end of rnd (18 sts).
Rnd 2: Knit.
Rnd 3: *Inc 1, k2*; repeat *to* to end of rnd (24 sts).
Rnd 4: Knit.
Rnd 5: *Inc 1, k3*; repeat *to* to end of rnd (30 sts).
Rnd 6: Knit.
Rnd 7: *Inc 1, k4*; repeat *to* to end of rnd (36 sts).
Rnd 8: Knit.
Rnd 9: *Inc 1, k5*; repeat *to* to end of rnd (42 sts).
Rnd 10: Knit, then turn work.
Rnd 11: Knit.
Rnd 12: Sl 1 st as if to purl, knit.
Rnds 13–15: Knit.
Rnd 16: *K5, ssk*; repeat *to* to end of rnd (36 sts).
Rnds 17–18: Knit.
Rnd 19: *K4, k2tog*; repeat *to* to end of rnd (30 sts).
Rnds 20–21: Knit.
Rnd 22: *K3, ssk*; repeat *to* to end of rnd (24 sts).
Rnds 23–24: Knit.
Rnd 25: *K2, k2tog*; repeat *to* to end of rnd (18 sts).
Rnds 26–27: Knit.
Rnd 28: *K1, ssk*; repeat *to* to end of rnd (12 sts).
Rnd 29: Knit.

(continued)

Rnd 30: *K2tog*; repeat *to* to end of rnd (6 sts).
Break Color E yarn, leaving a 6-inch/15-cm tail. Using a tapestry needle, thread tail through remaining 6 sts and tie off. Leave the hole at the bottom of the mushroom unsewn. Be sure the mushroom's cap is purl side out and everything else is knit side out. Close any holes and secure all loose ends left behind after turning your work or joining in new yarn colors.

Felting the Gnome and Mushroom

Machine felt the gnome and mushroom as directed on pages 4–7, using one or two Shout® ColorCatcher® sheet(s) in the washing machine. Red yarns can bleed and the sheet will trap the bleeding. Felt the gnome and mushroom for one to two cycles. Check on the gnome and mushroom periodically while they are felting, inserting your finger into the hat and the stem of the mushroom to keep those openings from felting shut. The last 2 inches/5 cm of the gnome's hat may felt shut, and that's okay. Felt until the knit stitches disappear and the gnome laid out flat measures about 7 to 8 inches/18 to 20 cm from its base to the tip of the hat, and the mushroom laid out flat measures about 7 inches/18 cm tall.

Tug and pull the wet gnome into your desired shape. Stuff his hat with fiberfill; the hat should be more flat-like front to back than rounded, with a slight curl at the tip. Stuff the body with fiberfill so it is more rounded than the hat. Tug and pull the gnome's shoes into shape, especially widthwise. Indent the gnome's base slightly so the body and shoes sit upright and flat, level with the table surface. If necessary, pin the tips of the shoes so they curl up slightly and allow the gnome to air dry completely in this position.

Tug and pull the wet mushroom into shape. Round out the cap and stem. Indent the bottom slightly so the mushroom will stand erect on a flat surface. The mushroom does not require fiberfill to retain its shape. Allow the mushroom to air dry completely in this position.

Assembling the Gnome

Once dry, pull the fiberfill out of the gnome's body only, leaving the hat's fiberfill intact.

SEWING THE COVERALL BUTTON(S)

A button or two can be sewn to the front of the gnome's coveralls by threading a chenille needle with a strand of any color yarn. Knot one end. Bury the knotted end on the inside of the gnome. Sew the button(s) onto the front of the coveralls, right above the shoes. Secure the thread on the inside wall by making a tiny stitch.

FILLING THE GNOME WITH POLY-PELLETS

Filling the gnome with poly-pellets will provide it with a more flexible base, allowing it to stand upright on a flat surface. Thread a chenille needle with a strand of Color A yarn, knotting one end. Sew a running stitch all along the outside edge of the opening at the base of the gnome as shown in Diagram 1. Leave the needle and yarn attached to the gnome. It will be used to sew the opening closed after the gnome is filled with poly-pellets.

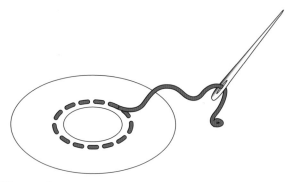

Diagram 1

Begin spooning poly-pellets into the opening. Occasionally push the poly-pellets down with your finger or the spoon handle to make room for more pellets. Fill the body with pellets until it is firm but still fairly squishy. If it is too firm, the gnome will wobble and not stand upright.

Once the poly-pellets are in, gently pull the yarn (still attached to gnome and needle) until the opening closes as tightly as possible, being careful not to break the yarn. With the chenille needle sew three to five stitches to completely close the opening so no poly-pellets can sneak out. Bury the loose end within the gnome.

MAKING THE GNOME'S NOSE AND EYES

To create his bobble-like nose, pull off a small piece of red roving. Roll it between the palms of your hands, creating a tiny ball. Position the ball in the center of the face area, directly up from the shoes. With the felting needle, begin poking all around the outer edges of the nose to adhere it to the face. Be careful not to poke the roving too much—you want to keep the nose raised, not flattened. Round out the nose's edges to keep it ball-like.

Thread a beading needle with a strand of the white bead thread. The thread is used to sew on the black bead eyes as well as to create a white highlight dot in each eye, giving them dimension. Insert the needle into the side of the gnome's head and come out in the first eye position, just next to the nose. Pull the thread just until its end slides inside the gnome. Sew two tiny stitches to anchor the thread. Place a bead on the needle and direct the needle back into the gnome at the same spot where the thread emerged. Direct the needle up to the second eye position. Pull the thread so the first bead lies taut against the wool face but not indented. Place the second bead on the needle and direct it into the gnome, the same spot where the thread emerged. Come out on another spot within the face area.

To end, sew a tiny stitch at this spot to secure the thread, small enough so it's not too visible. Direct the needle back into the head and out. Snip the loose thread.

NEEDLE FELTING THE GNOME'S BEARD

Pull off about a 4-inch/10-cm length of cream wool roving for the beard and slightly scrunch it up on one end. With the felting needle, poke the scrunched-up end of the roving, adhering it to the face about $1/4$ inch/.5 cm from one of the eyes and tucked under the hat brim. Once attached, scrunch up the other end and needle felt that to the face tucked under the hat brim, in same position from the other eye. (At this point, it may seem like way too much roving—don't worry, as you needle felt it, the gnome's beard will become smaller and slightly denser.)

Needle felt the roving under the nose and along both sides of the face just until it sticks and can't be tugged off. Poke the outer edges, keeping the beard long and tapering both sides. The beard's longest point should be just above the top (or only) button on the coveralls. Once the beard is completely tacked down, shape it, adding tufts and swirls with the felting needle. But be careful not to overwork the roving—the more it is poked, the denser it becomes.

If the beard becomes too dense or matted, fluff it up slightly using the tip of a chenille needle to gently lift it. Lifting the roving makes for a fuzzier and messier beard. To create a point or curl at the beard's end, gently pull the roving, twisting it as you pull.

Making Polka Dotted Mushrooms

Once dry, the mushroom is ready for embellishing. Pull off a small pinch of white roving and roll it between the palms of your hands to form a tiny ball. The size of each polka dot depends on how much roving you use and how much you roll it. Position the ball on the mushroom's cap. With the all-purpose felting needle, begin poking the outer edges of the ball, forming a round dot. Flatten the dot onto the cap with the needle until flush with the red wool. The dots can be left slightly raised or flattened completely. Continue applying dots of various sizes until the mushroom cap is evenly covered.

To finish, wet the dots with water. Wet your finger and smooth it over each polka dot. This softens the roving and eliminates any holes left behind by the felting needle.

Antiquing Your Gnome's Beard

Traditionally a gnome's beard is long and white. To make your gnome's beard more weathered-looking, dye the roving with brewed coffee. Coffee will turn the roving a slight tan-brown color, whereas brewed tea will give the roving an orange-rust color.

To coffee dye the roving, immerse it in a bowl of water until it is saturated. Let the roving soak for thirty minutes. Combine $1/4$ cup/60 ml instant coffee crystals and 4 cups water in a medium-size pan. Stirring the mixture, bring it to a boil over medium-high heat, then add 3 tablespoons/45 ml distilled white vinegar. Remove from the heat and allow it to cool slightly.

Once the mixture is tepid, submerge the wet roving into the coffee solution. Gently stir it to distribute the color evenly. The roving can be left in the dye anywhere from five minutes to overnight, depending on how dark you want the beard to be. Five minutes is plenty of time to soak your roving, giving it a hint of color but not making it too dark.

Once the roving has soaked for the desired time, lift it out of the coffee mixture. Thoroughly rinse the roving with water and gently wring out the excess. After rinsing, the roving will be one to two shades lighter than before rinsing. Allow the dyed roving to air dry completely. The roving is then ready for needle felting.

Matilda the Witch

*C*reate your own wickedly cute witch with hooked nose and chin—and don't forget her tiny broom!

Materials

NOTE: When choosing yarns, do not use a machine washable yarn (like superwash merino) as it will not felt. The colors and brands listed are for the witch shown in the photo opposite.

- Color A (dress, hat, and shoes): 43 yd./39.5 m black 100% wool #4 medium worsted weight yarn (shown using Brown Sheep Company Nature Spun Worsted, #601 Pepper, 245 yd./232 m per skein)
- Color B (face): 9 yd./8.5 m lime green 100% wool #4 medium worsted weight yarn (shown using Brown Sheep Company Nature Spun Worsted, #109 Spring Green, 100% wool, 245 yd./232 m per skein)
- US 10 1/2/6.5 mm set of double-pointed needles
- US 10 1/2/6.5 mm circular needles, any length, for picking up sts around the hat's brim
- Split-ring stitch marker
- Sharp tapestry needle
- Chenille needle
- Polyester fiberfill filling
- Plastic poly-pellets
- 1 button for dress, 1/2 inch/1.25 cm orange, yellow, or Halloween-themed button
- Lime green 100% wool roving to match Color B yarn, for nose and chin (*NOTE: If you can't find wool roving to match the skin color, you can create it from the Color B yarn; see directions for Adding the Features of Matilda's Face on page 60*)
- Pink 100% wool roving, for cheeks (optional)
- 38-gauge all-purpose felting needle
- Foam pad
- 2 black 4 mm round beads, for eyes
- John James size 11 straw bead needle, for eyes
- White bead thread, for eyes
- Black-purple curly mohair locks or Color A yarn, for hair
- 24-gauge black wire, for bats
- 1 sheet black acrylic felt, for bats
- Miniature whisk broom

Matilda the Witch

MATILDA'S DRESS

With Color A yarn and dpns, CO 12 sts. Divide the sts evenly among 3 dpns, taking care not to twist them. Join to work in the rnd.

Rnd 1: *Inc 1, k1*; repeat *to* to end of rnd. Place a stitch marker to indicate beg of rnd (18 sts).
Rnd 2: Knit.
Rnd 3: *Inc 1, k2*; repeat *to* to end of rnd (24 sts).
Rnd 4: Knit.
Rnd 5: *Inc 1, k3*; repeat *to* to end of rnd (30 sts), then turn work.
Rnd 6: Knit.
Rnd 7: Sl 1 st, knit to end of rnd.
Rnd 8: K1, p12, k17. These 12 purl sts will be picked up later for her two shoes.
Rnds 9–18: Knit.
Break Color A yarn, leaving a 6-inch/15-cm tail.

MATILDA'S FACE

Rnd 1: Join Color B yarn, knit.
Rnds 2–7: Knit.
Break Color B yarn, leaving a 6-inch/15-cm tail.

MATILDA'S HAT

Rnd 1: Join Color A yarn, knit.
Rnd 2: Purl. These purl sts will be picked up later for the brim of the hat.
Rnd 3: Knit.
Rnd 4: K2tog, k13, k2tog, k13 (28 sts).
Rnd 5: *K1, ssk, k8, k2tog, k1*; repeat *to* to end of rnd (24 sts).
Rnds 6–8: Knit.
Rnd 9: *K1, ssk, k6, k2tog, k1*; repeat *to* to end of rnd (20 sts).
Rnds 10–12: Knit.
Rnd 13: *K1, ssk, k4, k2tog, k1*; repeat *to* to end of rnd (16 sts).
Rnds 14–16: Knit.
Rnd 17: *K1, ssk, k2, k2tog, k1*; repeat *to* to end of rnd (12 sts).

(continued)

Rnd 18: K6 sts onto one dpn and 6 onto second dpn.

Rnds 19–20: Knit.

Rnd 21: *K1, ssk, k2tog, k1*; repeat *to* to end of rnd (8 sts).

Rnds 22–24: Knit.

Rnd 25: *K2tog*; repeat *to* until all sts are on one dpn (4 sts). Do not turn work. Slide the work to the right of the needle.

Rnd 26: Knit. Do not turn work. Slide the work to the right of the needle.

Rnds 27–31: Rep Rnd 26.

Break Color A yarn, leaving a 6-inch/15-cm tail. Using a tapestry needle, thread tail through remaining 4 sts and tie off.

BRIM OF MATILDA'S HAT

With the circular needle, pick up the bottom loop of each purl st around the base of the hat for a total of 30 sts.

With two strands of Color A yarn and dpns, CO 3 sts. Do not turn work. This additional strand of yarn will create a thicker, wider hat brim after felting. Begin knitting the I-cord bind-off as follows: Slide the 3 sts from the dpn onto the tip of left circular needle. With the dpn, knit the first 2 sts off, and then slip the next st as if to knit. Knit another st from the circular needle and pass the slipped st over the previously knitted st and off the needle. Slide these 3 sts from the dpn back onto the circular needle. Repeat this process until only 3 sts remain on the dpn. Break Color A yarn, leaving a 6-inch/15-cm tail. Using a tapestry needle, thread tail through remaining 3 sts from right to left and tie off. Sew both I-cord ends to Matilda's hat, overlapping them slightly so they appear as one continuous cord.

MATILDA'S SHOES

With Color A yarn, complete Matilda's shoes according to the Woodland Gnome pattern (see page 54).

Felting and Assembling Matilda the Witch

Machine felt Matilda, sew on her decorative yellow or orange buttons, and then fill her with poly-pellets according to the Woodland Gnome pattern. Once felted and dry, you can embellish Matilda's hat by feather stitching (see page 21 for a tutorial) around the base of her hat as shown in the photo on page 58.

ADDING THE FEATURES OF MATILDA'S FACE

Once Matilda is dry, you will add a protruding hooked nose and chin using the lime green wool roving. (If you can't find wool roving to match the skin color, you can create it from the lime green worsted weight yarn. Cut several 1-inch/2.5-cm pieces. Pull the plies apart and rub them between your fingers to create enough little balls of roving for needle felting a nose and chin.)

Place a small pinch of roving on the foam pad and begin poking it with the felting needle, rotating it constantly so it doesn't become flattened or stuck to the pad. You want to create a round protruding knob that will

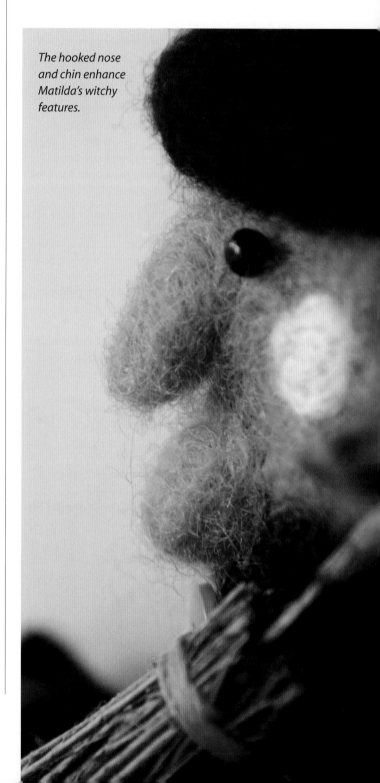

The hooked nose and chin enhance Matilda's witchy features.

be the chin. Its exact size will be determined by the size of your gnome, adding more roving if needed. It should protrude from the face at least $^1/_2$ inch/1.25 cm, as shown in the photo opposite. When you're satisfied with the chin's size and shape, position it on her face, and poke all around the edges, adhering it to the wool underneath. Make a nose the same way (and add a wart if you like!). Attach the nose to the face just above the chin with a slight gap in between. You can use more yarn fluff to fill in any holes or cracks, and to blend both the chin and nose smoothly to the face. After the chin and nose are in position, they can be shaped further, adding details such as nostrils or a wart, but it isn't necessary.

To give Matilda rosy cheeks, roll a tiny pinch of the pink roving into a tiny ball. Needle felt the ball until it lies flat against her face. Sew on the eyes as for the Woodland Gnome pattern.

ADDING MATILDA'S HAIR

There are two hair choices: black dyed curly mohair locks, as shown in the photo on page 58, or black worsted or bulky weight yarn.

Curly Locks Hair

Pull off a single lock of the mohair locks and needle felt one end of it onto Matilda, at the back of her head just under the brim of her hat. Continue adding locks all along the brim's underside in the same way, stopping on either side of her cheeks. Once all the locks are basted into place, needle felt them again so they can't be tugged off. When they are all securely attached, gently rub them between your fingers to fluff, creating a full, wild look.

Yarn Hair

If using yarn, cut several 4-inch/10-cm lengths of black worsted or bulky yarn. Fold one length in half and insert the folded end into the eye of a sharp tapestry needle. Insert the needle into the back of the head just under the brim of the hat. Direct the needle out and stop when the folded yarn end pops out. Remove the needle, and insert the two yarn ends through the loop and pull snugly. Repeat this all along the edge of the hat brim, stopping on either side of Matilda's cheeks. Attach enough strands to create a full head of hair. Don't worry if the strands are uneven at this point. Add a strand or two of purple here and there if you want to give the hair colored streaks. Once you've attached all the yarn strands, pull their individual plies apart and rub the plies together between your fingers to frizz her hair. Trim the frizzy ends to desired length or leave unruly.

MAKING MATILDA'S FLYING BATS

Using the template in Diagram 1, cut out the bat from a piece of black felt. Cut out at least one more bat. Cut a 12-inch/31-cm length of black 24-gauge wire. Insert one end of the wire up through one of the bats, then immediately back down through it. Twist the two ends together. The other bat is attached to the same wire as the first bat by poking the end of the wire through the new bat. To hold the bat in place, create a slight loop in the wire by wrapping it around a US 10$^1/_2$/6.5 mm dpn. To finish, poke the wire's end into Matilda's hat about 3 inches/7.5 cm, until the wire stands up by itself, leaving enough room for the bats to be flying around Matilda's head (see page 58). Adjust the wire length by trimming it if it appears too long and the bats are flying too far away.

 **Actual size**

Diagram 1

ADDING MATILDA'S BROOM

A small whisk broom can be found in any craft store selling miniature dollhouse items. You can tack the broom onto Matilda using a few small stitches or simply prop it up against her once you stand her up for display.

Your witch is now ready for her first flying lesson!

Jolly St. Nick

This jolly little Santa is the perfect size to tuck inside a wreath or holiday stocking. You'll find him poking his little head out to greet you on Christmas morning!

Materials

NOTE: When choosing yarns, do not use a machine washable yarn (like superwash merino) as it will not felt. Also, white yarns generally don't felt well. For a list of cream and other off-white yarns that do felt reliably, see page 2. The colors and brands listed are for the Santa shown in the photo opposite.

- Color A (coveralls, hat, and shoes): 38 yd./35 m red 100% wool #4 medium worsted weight yarn (shown using Brown Sheep Company Nature Spun Worsted, #N46 Red Fox, 245 yd./232 m per skein)
- Color B (face and hat brim): 14 yd./13 m cream 100% wool #4 medium worsted weight yarn (shown using Brown Sheep Company Nature Spun Worsted, #N91 Aran, 245 yd./232 m per skein)
- Color C (hat brim novelty trim, optional): 4 yd./4 m white Trendsetter Aura novelty yarn, #3110 White, 100% nylon, 145 yd./133 m per skein (Use this if you'd like to add a sparkly fluffy white brim to Santa's hat—if you cannot locate this yarn, you can also create a fluffy white brim using white roving. Once felted and completely dry, needle felt the roving to the brim of Santa's hat.)
- US 10¹/₂/6.5 mm set of double-pointed needles
- US 10¹/₂/6.5 mm circular needles, any length, for picking up sts around the hat's brim
- Split-ring stitch marker
- Tapestry needle
- Chenille needle
- Polyester fiberfill filling
- Plastic poly-pellets
- 2 white buttons, for backside of coveralls
- Red 100% wool roving, for nose
- Pink 100% wool roving, for cheeks (optional)
- 2 black 4 mm round beads, for eyes
- John James size 11 straw bead needle, for eyes
- White bead thread, for eyes
- White mohair curly locks, for beard
- White 100% wool roving, for hat's pom-pom
- 38-gauge all-purpose felting needle
- Foam pad

Jolly St. Nick

ST. NICK'S COVERALLS

With Color A yarn and dpns, CO 12 sts. Divide the sts evenly among 3 dpns, taking care not to twist them. Join to work in the rnd.

Rnd 1: *Inc , k1*; repeat *to* to end of rnd. Place a stitch marker to indicate beg of rnd (18 sts).
Rnd 2: Knit.
Rnd 3: *Inc 1, k2*; repeat *to* to end of rnd (24 sts).
Rnd 4: Knit.
Rnd 5: *Inc 1, k3*; repeat *to* to end of rnd (30 sts), then turn work.
Rnd 6: Knit.
Rnd 7: Sl 1 st, knit to end of rnd.
Rnd 8: K1, p12, k17. These 12 purl sts will be picked up later for the Santa's two shoes.
Rnds 9–18: Knit.
Break Color A yarn, leaving a 6-inch/15-cm tail.

ST. NICK'S FACE

Rnd 1: Join Color B yarn, knit.
Rnds 2–7: Knit.

ST. NICK'S HAT

Rnd 1: Knit.
Rnd 2: Purl. Break Color B yarn, leaving a 6-inch/15-cm tail. These purl sts will be picked up later for the brim of the Santa's hat.
Rnd 3: Join Color A yarn, knit.
Rnd 4: K2tog, k13, k2tog, k13 (28 sts).
Rnd 5: *K1, ssk, k8, k2tog, k1*; repeat *to* to end of rnd (24 sts).
Rnds 6–8: Knit.
Rnd 9: *K1, ssk, k6, k2tog, k1*; repeat *to* to end of rnd (20 sts).
Rnds 10–12: Knit.
Rnd 13: *K1, ssk, k4, k2tog, k1*; repeat *to* to end of rnd (16 sts).

(continued)

Tuck a holiday St. Nick gnome inside a wreath and hang it as a jolly greeting to all your welcomed guests!

Rnds 14–16: Knit.

Rnd 17: *K1, ssk, k2, k2tog, k1*; repeat *to* to end of rnd (12 sts).

Rnd 18: K6 sts onto one dpn and 6 onto second dpn.

Rnds 19–20: Knit.

Rnd 21: *K1, ssk, k2tog, k1*; repeat *to* to end of rnd (8 sts).

Rnds 22–24: Knit.

Rnd 25: *K2tog*; repeat *to* until all sts are on one dpn (4 sts). Do not turn work. Slide work to right of needle.

Rnd 26: Knit. Do not turn work. Slide the work to the right of the needle.

Rnds 27–31: Rep Rnd 26.

Break Color A yarn, leaving a 6-inch/15-cm tail. Using a tapestry needle, thread tail through remaining 4 sts and tie off.

BRIM OF ST. NICK'S HAT

With the circular needle, pick up the bottom loop of each purl st around the base of the hat for a total of 30 sts.

If using the sparkly novelty yarn Aura (Color C) or something similar, add it together with Color B yarn and on dpns, CO 3 sts. If not using the novelty yarn, then knit the brim with one strand of Color B yarn. Do not turn work. Begin knitting the I-cord bind-off as follows: Slide the 3 sts from the dpn onto the tip of left circular needle. With the dpn, knit the first 2 sts off, and then slip the next st as if to knit. Knit another st from the circular needle and pass the slipped st over the previously knitted st and off the needle. Slide these 3 sts from the dpn back onto the circular needle. Repeat this process until only 3 sts remain on the dpn. Break Colors B and C, leaving a 6-inch/15-cm tail. Using a tapestry needle, thread tail through remaining

3 sts from right to left and tie off. Sew both I-cord ends to the Santa's hat, overlapping them slightly so they appear as one continuous cord.

ST. NICK'S SHOES

With Color A yarn, complete St. Nick's shoes according to the Woodland Gnome pattern (see page 54).

Felting and Assembling Jolly St. Nick

Machine felt St. Nick, sew on the white buttons on his backside as shown in the photo, and fill him with poly-pellets according to the Woodland Gnome pattern (see page 56).

MAKING ST. NICK'S FACE AND BEARD

Once dry, add facial features (his nose and eyes) according to the Woodland Gnome pattern (see page 56). Once the eyes and nose are in position, if you want to give St. Nick rosy cheeks, roll a tiny pinch of the pink roving into a ball. Needle felt the ball until it lies flat against his face. Repeat for his other cheek.

For the beard, pull off a single clump of curls of the mohair locks and needle felt one end of it onto his face just under the brim of his hat starting on either side of his face and making sure his rosy cheeks still peek out from under the curls. Continue adding locks until the beard is full and thick. Once all the locks are basted into place, needle felt them again so they can't be tugged off. When they are all securely attached, gently rub the locks between your fingers to fluff them up.

MAKING THE POM-POM FOR ST. NICK'S CAP

Roll a good-size pinch of white roving between your palms into a ball; the larger the pinch of roving, the larger the pom-pom will be. On a foam pad, needle felt the roving into a firm round ball, rotating it so it doesn't flatten or stick to the pad. Sew the pom-pom to the tip of the hat with a strand of the red yarn and a chenille needle, securing it firmly to the hat. Bury the end within the hat. With the tip of the chenille needle, gently fluff up the ball to create a wispy-looking pom-pom.

The two white buttons on St. Nick's backside give the look of a pair of red coveralls.

Lucky the Leprechaun

According to Irish folklore, a leprechaun is a male faerie and most of them are cobblers. They are known to be mischievous and love to bury their treasures. Don't wait for a rainbow to appear to make your very own leprechaun!

Materials

NOTE: When choosing yarns, do not use a machine wash-able yarn (like superwash merino) as it will not felt. Also, white yarns generally don't felt well. For a list of cream and other off-white yarns that do felt reliably, see page 2. The colors and brands listed are for the leprechaun shown in the photo opposite.

- Color A (coveralls, hat, and shoes): 43 yd./39.5 m green 100% wool #4 medium worsted weight yarn (shown using Brown Sheep Company Nature Spun Worsted, #156 Irish Shamrock, 245 yd./232 m per skein)
- Color B (face): 9 yd./8.5 m cream 100% wool #4 medium worsted weight yarn (shown using Brown Sheep Company Nature Spun Worsted, #N91 Aran, 245 yd./232 m per skein)
- US 10¹/₂/6.5 mm set of double-pointed needles
- US 10¹/₂/6.5 mm circular needles, any length, for picking up sts around the hat's brim
- Split-ring stitch marker
- Tapestry needle
- Chenille needle
- Polyester fiberfill filling
- Plastic poly-pellets
- 1 or 2 gold or silver button(s), for coveralls
- Orange 100% wool roving, for beard
- 38-gauge all-purpose felting needle
- Foam pad
- Red 100% wool roving, for nose
- 2 black 4 mm round beads, for eyes
- Size 11 John James straw bead needle, for eyes
- White bead thread
- 10-inch/25-cm length of ¹/₂-inch/1.25-cm black pleather or satin ribbon, for hatband
- Buckle-like button (1 inch/2.5 cm square), for hatband
- 1 square bright green acrylic felt, for shamrock
- Sharp-ended toothpick, for pipe
- ¹/₂-inch/1.25-cm cork, for pipe

Lucky the Leprechaun

LUCKY'S COVERALLS

With Color A yarn and dpns, CO 12 sts. Divide the sts evenly among 3 dpns, taking care not to twist them. Join to work in the rnd.

Rnd 1: *Inc , k1*; repeat *to* to end of rnd. Place a stitch marker to indicate beg of rnd (18 sts).

Rnd 2: Knit.

Rnd 3: *Inc 1, k2*; repeat *to* to end of rnd (24 sts).

Rnd 4: Knit.

Rnd 5: *Inc 1, k3*; repeat *to* to end of rnd (30 sts), then turn work.

Rnd 6: Knit.

Rnd 7: Sl 1 st, knit to end of rnd.

Rnd 8: K1, p12, k17. These 12 purl sts will be picked up later for the Leprechaun's two shoes.

Rnds 9–18: Knit.

Break Color A yarn, leaving a 6-inch/15-cm tail.

LUCKY'S FACE

Rnd 1: Join Color B yarn, knit.

Rnds 2–7: Knit.

Break Color B yarn, leaving a 6-inch/15-cm tail.

LUCKY'S HAT

Rnd 1: Join Color A yarn, knit.

Rnd 2: Purl. These purl sts will be picked up later for the brim of Lucky's hat.

Rnd 3: Knit.

Rnd 4: K2tog, k13, k2tog, k13 (28 sts).

Rnd 5: *K1, ssk, k8, k2tog, k1*; repeat *to* to end of rnd (24 sts).

Rnds 6–8: Knit.

Rnd 9: *K1, ssk, k6, k2tog, k1*; repeat *to* to end of rnd (20 sts).

Rnds 10–12: Knit.

Rnd 13: *K1, ssk, k4, k2tog, k1*; repeat *to* to end of rnd (16 sts).

(continued)

Rnds 14–16: Knit.

Rnd 17: *K1, ssk, k2, k2tog, k1*; repeat *to* to end of rnd (12 sts).

Rnd 18: K6 sts onto one dpn and 6 onto second dpn.

Rnds 19–20: Knit.

Rnd 21: *K1, ssk, k2tog, k1*; repeat *to* to end of rnd (8 sts).

Rnds 22–24: Knit.

Rnd 25: *K2tog*; repeat *to* until all sts are on one dpn (4 sts). Do not turn work. Slide work to right of needle.

Rnd 26: Knit. Do not turn work. Slide the work to the right of the needle.

Rnds 27–31: Rep Rnd 26.

Break Color A yarn, leaving a 6-inch/15-cm tail. Using a tapestry needle, thread tail through remaining 4 sts and tie off.

BRIM OF LUCKY'S HAT

With the circular needle, pick up the bottom loop of each purl st around the base of the hat for a total of 30 sts.

With two strands of Color A yarn and dpns, CO 3 sts. This additional strand of yarn will create a thicker and wider hat brim after felting. Do not turn work. Begin knitting the I-cord bind-off as follows: Slide the 3 sts from the dpn onto the tip of left circular needle. With the dpn, knit the first 2 sts off, and then slip the next st as if to knit. Knit another st from the circular needle and pass the slipped st over the previously knitted st and off the needle. Slide these 3 sts from the dpn back onto the circular needle. Repeat this process until only 3 sts remain on the dpn. Break Color A yarn, leaving a 6-inch/15-cm tail. Using a tapestry needle, thread tail through remaining 3 sts from right to left and tie off. Sew both I-cord ends to the gnome's hat, overlapping them slightly so they appear as one continuous cord.

LUCKY'S SHOES

With Color A yarn, complete Lucky's shoes according to the Woodland Gnome pattern (see page 54).

A leprechaun would never feel completely dressed without a little shamrock adorning his coveralls!

Felting and Assembling Lucky the Leprechaun

Machine felt Lucky and, once dry, sew on his gold decorative buttons, and then fill him with stuffing and poly-pellets according to the Woodland Gnome pattern (see page 56). Add his facial features (nose and eyes) and an orange roving beard.

MAKING LUCKY'S HATBAND AND BUCKLE

Create a decorative band for the hat using the black pleather or satin ribbon. Wrap it around the hat just at the brim. Insert one end through the buckle-like button. Trim the end so it tucks behind the buckle's front. Weave the other end through the opposite side of the buckle and over the first end. Adjust the band to fit. Trim any excess so both ends are concealed behind the buckle.

MAKING LUCKY'S SHAMROCK

Needle felt a felt shamrock leaf onto your leprechaun's behind for extra good luck. Using the template in Diagram 1, trace and then cut out a shamrock from the green felt.

   With the felting needle, poke the shamrock to the gnome's backside, until it adheres and lies smooth and flat against the wool underneath. Wet the shamrock and smooth your wet finger over it to soften the felt and eliminate any holes the felting needle left behind.

Actual size

Diagram 1

MAKING LUCKY'S CORNCOB PIPE

To make a corncob pipe, poke one end of a sharp-ended toothpick into the side of the cork. Ease the toothpick end of the pipe into the beard about where a mouth would be.

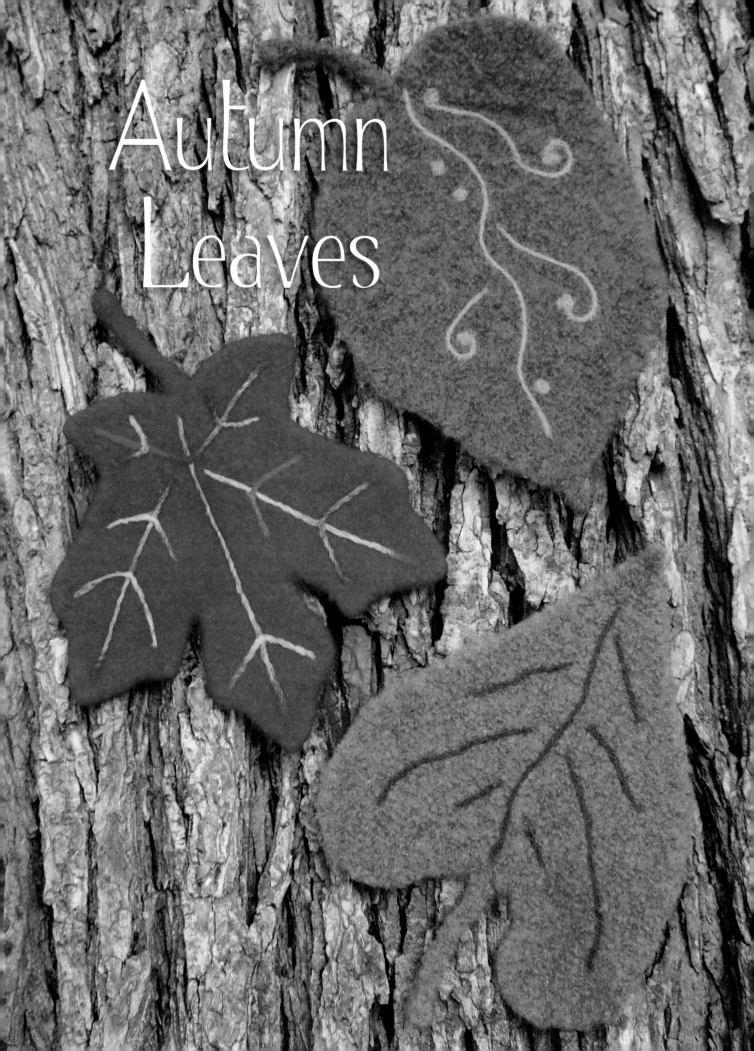

Autumn Leaves

U se these leaves as whimsical candle rugs or autumnal trivets. Or create an autumn display with these larger-than-life felted leaves scattered about your dining room table! Each embellished leaf is truly a work of functional art! Included are directions for making maple, elm, and linden leaves, in both small and large sizes.

Felted Measurements

From end to end, not including stem.
Elm Leaf, small: 7 inches/18 cm
Elm Leaf, large: 9^1/$_2$ inches/24 cm
Maple Leaf, small: 6 inches/15 cm
Maple Leaf, large: 7^1/$_2$ inches/19 cm
Linden Leaf, small: 7^1/$_2$ inches/20 cm
Linden Leaf, large: 8^1/$_2$ inches/20.5 cm

Materials

NOTE: When choosing yarns, do not use a machine wash-able yarn (like superwash merino) as it will not felt.

Small Leaf

- Elm: 45 yd./41.5 m green 100% wool #2 sport weight yarn
- Maple: 29 yd./26.5 m red 100% wool #2 sport weight yarn
- Linden: 43 yd./39.5 m green 100% wool #2 sport weight yarn
- US 8/5 mm set of double-pointed needles
- US 8/5 mm circular needles, 16 inches/40.5 cm long

Large Leaf

- Elm: 52 yd./47.5 m green 100% wool #3 medium or #4 worsted weight yarn
- Maple: 49 yd./45 m red 100% wool #3 medium or #4 worsted weight yarn
- Linden: 59 yd./54 m green 100% wool #3 medium or #4 worsted weight yarn
- US 10^1/$_2$/6.5 mm set of double-pointed needles
- US 10^1/$_2$/6.5 mm circular needles, 24 inches/61 cm long

Both Sizes

- Small stitch holder
- Split-ring stitch markers
- Tapestry needle

For optional embellishments

- 100% wool yarn of any weight or wool roving in coordinating or contrasting colors for leaf veins
- 38-gauge all-purpose felting needle
- Large foam pad
- Purple quilter's pen, for drawing vein lines
- Soft-bristle toothbrush
- Pieces of green felt, for appliqué project
- Scissors
- Embroidery floss in colors to coordinate with felt and leaf yarn, for appliqué project

Two sizes of maple leaves are shown here with and without added vein lines. Keep the final designs simple!

On preceding page: *The large maple leaf was knit with Brown Sheep Nature Spun Worsted #N46 Red Fox. The elm leaf was knit with Nature Spun Worsted #144 Limestone and the linden leaf with Ella Rae Classic Worsted #108 Mustard.*

Notes

- For all three types of leaves, to make the small size, use #2 sport weight yarn and smaller needles; for the large size, use #3 medium or #4 worsted weight yarn and the larger needles.
- The wraps and turns (w&t) are used for creating short rows, to help with shaping the leaf.

Special Stitches

inc 1: Increase one stitch by knitting into the front and then back of same stitch.

M1: Increase one stitch by making a loop cast-on to the right hand needle.

ssk: Slip, slip, knit. Slip one stitch as if to knit onto the right needle, then slip another in the same way. Insert the left needle into the front of the two slipped stitches. Knit these stitches together; this creates a left-slanting decrease.

p2togTBL: Slip the two stitches knitwise, one at a time, to the right needle. Return these stitches to the left needle, keeping them twisted. Then purl the two stitches together through the back loops; this creates a right-slanting decrease on knit side.

w&t (k): Wrap & turn knit side. Knit up to the turning point, slip the next stitch purlwise onto the right needle, bring the yarn forward between the needles, return the slipped stitch to the left needle, pass the yarn between the needles to the back of the work, turn work to the purl side and begin purling.

w&t (p): Wrap & turn purl side. Purl up to the turning point, slip the next stitch purlwise onto the right needle, bring the yarn to the back between the needles, return the slipped stitch to the left needle, pass the yarn between the needles to the front of the work, turn work to the knit side and begin knitting.

Elm Leaf

This is worked from the bottom up to the tip, then a few stitches are picked up at the bottom of the leaf and a simple I-cord is knit to create a stem.

ELM LEAF BODY

With circular needles, loosely CO 6 sts.
Row 1 (RS): K1, inc 1, k1, inc 1, inc 1, k1 (9 sts).
Row 2 (WS): Purl to end, M1 (10 sts).
Row 3: K1, inc 1, k5, inc 1, inc 1, k1 (13 sts).
Row 4: Purl.
Row 5: K1, inc 1, k8, inc 1, inc 1, k1 (16 sts).
Row 6: Purl.
Row 7: Knit to last 2 sts, inc 1, k1 (17 sts).

The elm leaves were knit using Brown Sheep's Nature Spun #144 Limestone in sport weight for the smaller leaf and worsted weight for the larger. The larger leaf has needle-felted vein designs, and the smaller leaf's veins were embroidered with a running stitch using worsted weight yarn.

Row 8: Purl to end, place a stitch marker below last stitch to mark for stem, then [M1] 4 times (21 sts).
Row 9: K1, inc 1, knit to end (22 sts).
Row 10: Purl to end, M1 (23 sts).
Row 11: Knit.
Row 12: Purl to end, M1 (24 sts).
Row 13: Knit to last 2 sts, inc 1, k1 (25 sts).
Row 14: Purl to end, M1 (26 sts).
Row 15: Knit.
Row 16: Purl to end, M1 (27 sts).
Row 17: Knit to last 2 sts, inc 1, k1 (28 sts).
Row 18: Purl to end, M1 (29 sts).
Row 19: Knit.
Row 20: Purl.
Row 21: K1, inc 1, knit to last 2 sts, inc 1, k1 (31 sts).
Row 22: Purl.
Row 23: Knit.
Row 24: Purl.
Row 25: K1, inc 1, knit to end (32 sts).
Row 26: Purl.
Row 27: Knit.
Row 28: Purl.
Rows 29–46: [Rep Rows 27–28] 9 times.
Row 47: Ssk, knit to last 2 sts, k2tog (30 sts).

Row 48: Purl.
Rows 49–60: [Rep Rows 47–48] 6 times (18 sts).
Row 61: Ssk, knit to last 2 sts, k2tog (16 sts).
Row 62: P2tog, purl to last 2 sts, p2togTBL (14 sts).
Rows 63–66: [Rep Rows 61–62] 2 times (6 sts).
Row 67: Ssk, k2tog, k2tog (3 sts).
Row 68: Purl.
Row 69: K1, k2tog (2 sts).
Row 70: Purl.
Row 71: Knit.
Row 72: Purl.
Row 73: K2tog (1 st).
Break yarn, leaving a 6-inch/15-cm tail. Thread tail
   through the remaining stitch and tie off.

ELM LEAF STEM

Position the leaf so its knit side is facing up. At the stitch
   marker using two dpns, pick up and knit 2 sts at the
   leaf's edge. Do not turn work. Slide the work to the
   right of the needle. Remove stitch marker.
Rows 1–15: Knit. Do not turn work. Slide the work to the
   right of the needle.
Row 16: [Inc 1] 2 times (4 sts). Do not turn work. Slide the
   work to the right of the needle.
Row 17: Knit. Do not turn work. Slide the work to the
   right of the needle.
Row 18: [K2tog] 2 times (2 sts). Slide the work to the right
   of the needle.
Break yarn, leaving a 6-inch/15-cm tail. With a tapestry
   needle, thread the tail through the remaining 2 sts
   right to left and tie off. Direct the threaded tapestry
   needle in and out of the stem's end two or three times,
   creating a slight ball. Secure all loose ends.
If you're adding decorative vein lines that need to be
   applied before felting (see pages 76–78), do it now.

Maple Leaf

This leaf is the most intricate of the three. You will do a
long-tail cast-on and work up, dividing the stitches at a
certain point to work the three upper lobes of the maple
leaf. Once that is completed, you will pull out the cast-on
and work the lower two lobes of the leaf and the stem. To
get the wonderful tapering of the lobes, you will be using
short rows.

MAPLE LEAF BODY

With circular needle and scrap yarn, loosely CO 20 sts.
Knit 1 row.
Break yarn, leaving a 6-inch/15-cm tail. You will later pull
   this yarn out to create live stitches to pick up and knit
   the leaf's bottom edge and stem. Join the yarn again.
Row 1 (RS): Knit.
Row 2 (WS): Purl.
Rows 3–4: Rep Rows 1–2.
Row 5: K1, inc 1, knit to last 2 sts, inc 1, k1 (2 sts inc'd).
Row 6: Purl.
Rows 7–22: [Rep Rows 5–6] 8 times (38 sts).
Row 23: Ssk, knit to last 2 sts, k2tog (36 sts).

(continued)

*The felted leaves make wonderful decorative candle rugs for
your harvest table.*

Row 24: P2tog, purl to last 2 sts, p2togTBL (34 sts).
Row 25: Knit.
Row 26: Purl.
Row 27: K1, inc 1, knit to last 2 sts, inc 1, k1 (36 sts).
Row 28: Purl.
Row 29: Knit.
Row 30: Purl.
Row 31: K1, inc 1, knit to last 2 sts, inc 1, k1 (38 sts).

WORK LEFT SIDE LOBE

Row 1 (WS): P12, p2togTBL (13 sts), turn work.
Row 2 (RS): Knit.
Row 3: P11, p2togTBL (12 sts), turn work.
Row 4: Knit to last 2 sts, inc 1, k1 (13 sts).
Row 5: Loosely BO 8 sts pwise, p2, p2togTBL (4 sts), turn work.
Row 6: Sl 1, k3.
Row 7: P2, p2togTBL (3 sts).
Row 8: Sl 1, k2.
Row 9: P3tog (1 st).
Break yarn, leaving a 6-inch/15-cm tail. Thread tail through the remaining stitch and tie off.

WORK RIGHT SIDE LOBE

With the leaf's knit side facing you, join yarn.
Row 1 (RS): K12, k2tog (13 sts), turn work.
Row 2 (WS): Purl.
Row 3: K11, k2tog (12 sts), turn work.
Row 4: Purl to end, M1 (13 sts).
Row 5: Loosely BO 8 sts, k2, k2tog (4 sts), turn work.
Row 6: Sl 1, p3.
Row 7: K2, k2tog (3 sts).
Row 8: Sl 1, p2.
Row 9: K3tog (1 st).
Break yarn, leaving a 6-inch/15-cm tail. Thread tail through the remaining stitch and tie off.

WORK CENTER LOBE

With the leaf's knit side facing, join yarn.
Row 1: K1, inc 1, k6, inc 1, k1 (12 sts).
Row 2: Purl.
Row 3: Knit.
Rows 4–5: Rep Rows 2–3.
Row 6: Purl.
Row 7: K1, inc 1, k8, inc 1, k1 (14 sts).
Rows 8–11: [Rep Rows 2–3] 2 times.
Row 12: Purl.
Row 13: Ssk, k10, k2tog (12 sts).
Row 14: P2tog, p8, p2togTBL (10 sts).
Row 15: Ssk, k6, k2tog (8 sts).
Row 16: Purl.

Row 17: Ssk, k4, k2tog (6 sts).
Row 18: Purl.
Row 19: Knit.
Row 20: P2tog, p2, p2togTBL (4 sts).
Row 21: Knit.
Row 22: P2tog, p2togTBL (2 sts).
Row 23: Sl 1, k1, psso (1 st).
Break yarn, leaving a 6-inch/15-cm tail. Thread tail through the remaining stitch and tie off.

MAPLE LEAF BOTTOM

Position the leaf so its knit side and the scrap yarn edge are facing up. Starting on the right, gently cut the scrap yarn and pull it off. Transfer the 20 live stitches one at a time onto a needle, taking care not to twist them.
With the leaf's knit side and bottom edge facing up, join yarn.
Row 1: Knit.
Row 2: Purl.
Row 3: K1, inc 1, knit to last 2 sts, inc 1, k1 (22 sts).
Row 4: Purl.
Row 5: K1, inc 1, knit to last 2 sts, inc 1, k1 (24 sts).
Row 6: P9, w&t(p), k4, w&t(k), p3, w&t(p), k7, inc 1 (25 sts).
Row 7: Loosely BO 12 sts pwise, purl to end (13 sts).
Row 8: K9, w&t(k), p4, w&t(p), k3, w&t(k), purl to end, M1 (14 sts).
Row 9: Loosely BO 12 sts kwise, k1 (2 sts).
Transfer sts to a dpn. Do not turn work. Slide the work to the right of the needle.

MAPLE LEAF STEM

Rows 1–15: Knit. Do not turn work. Slide the work to the right of the needle.
Row 16: [Inc 1] 2 times (4 sts). Do not turn work. Slide the work to the right of the needle.
Row 17: Knit. Do not turn work. Slide the work to the right of the needle.
Row 18: [K2tog] 2 times (2 sts). Slide the work to the right of the needle.
Break yarn, leaving a 6-inch/15-cm tail. With a tapestry needle, thread the tail through the remaining 2 stitches, right to left and tie off. Direct the threaded tapestry needle in and out of the stem's end two or three times, creating a slight ball. Secure all loose ends.
If you're adding decorative vein lines that need to be applied before felting (see pages 76–78), do it now.

Linden Leaf

This leaf is worked from the top down and a few stitches will be picked up near the bottom for an I-cord stem.

LINDEN LEAF BODY

With circular needle, CO 2 sts.
Row 1: Purl.
Row 2: Knit.
Row 3: Purl.
Row 4: [Inc 1] 2 times (4 sts).
Row 5: Purl.
Row 6: K1, [Inc 1] 2 times, k1 (6 sts).
Row 7: Purl.
Row 8: K1, inc 1, k2, inc 1, k1 (8 sts).
Row 9: Purl.
Row 10: K1, inc 1, k4, inc 1, k1 (10 sts).
Row 11: Purl.
Row 12: K1, inc 1, knit to last 2 sts, inc 1, k1 (12 sts).
Row 13: Purl.
Rows 14–31: [Repeat Rows 12 and 13] 9 times (30 sts).
Row 32: Knit.
Row 33: Purl.
Row 34: K1, inc 1, knit to last 2 sts, inc 1, k1 (32 sts).
Row 35: Purl.
Row 36: Knit.
Row 37: Purl.
Row 38: K1, inc 1, knit to last 2 sts, inc 1, k1 (34 sts).
Row 39: Purl.
Row 40: Knit.
Row 41: Purl.
Row 42: K1, inc 1, knit to last 2 sts, inc 1, k1 (36 sts).
Row 43: Purl.
Row 44: Knit.
Row 45: Purl.
Rows 46–57: [Rep Rows 44–45] 6 times.
Row 58: Ssk, knit to end (35 sts).
Row 59: Purl.
Row 60: Ssk, knit to end (34 sts).

WORK LEFT LOBE OF LEAF

Row 1: P14, p2togTBL (15 sts), turn work.
Row 2: Ssk, knit to end (14 sts).
Row 3: P12, p2togTBL (13 sts), turn work.
Row 4: Inc 1, knit to last 2 sts, k2tog (13 sts).
Row 5: P13, turn work.
Row 6: Knit to last 2 sts, k2tog (12 sts).
Row 7: P12, turn work.
Row 8: Ssk, k8, k2tog (10 sts).
Row 9: P2tog, p6, p2togTBL (8 sts), turn work.
Row 10: Ssk, k4, k2tog (6 sts).
Row 11: [P2tog] 2 times, p2togTBL (3 sts), turn work.
Row 12: Loosely BO sts (1 st).
Break yarn, leaving a 6-inch/15-cm tail. Thread tail through the remaining stitch and tie off.

The linden leaf shape makes for the sweetest heart for that special valentine when knit using red yarns. No need for further embellishing here!

This linden leaf was embellished using simple vein lines adhered after felting with yarn scraps and a felting needle.

WORK RIGHT LOBE OF LEAF

With the leaf's right side facing you, join yarn.

Row 1: K11, [k2tog] 2 times (13 sts). Place the next 3 sts onto a stitch holder, turn work.

Row 2: P2tog, purl to last 2 sts, p2togTBL (11 sts).

Row 3: Knit to last 2 sts, k2tog (10 sts).

Rows 4–5: [Rep Rows 2–3] (7 sts).

Row 6: P2tog, p3, p2togTBL (5 sts).

Row 7: Ssk, loosely BO 3 sts (1 st).

Break yarn, leaving a 6-inch/15-cm tail. Thread tail through the remaining stitch and tie off.

LINDEN LEAF STEM

Transfer the 3 sts from stitch holder to a dpn. With the leaf's knit side facing you, join yarn.

Row 1: Knit. Do not turn work. Slide the work to the right of the needle.

Row 2: K1, k2tog (2 sts). Do not turn work. Slide the work to the right of the needle.

Rows 3–17: Knit. Do not turn work. Slide the work to the right of the needle.

Row 18: [Inc 1] 2 times (4 sts). Do not turn work. Slide the work to the right of the needle.

Row 19: Knit. Do not turn work. Slide the work to the right of the needle.

Row 20: [K2tog] 2 times (2 sts). Do not turn work. Slide the work to the right of the needle.

Break yarn, leaving a 6-inch/15-cm tail. With a tapestry needle, thread the tail through the remaining 2 stitches, right to left and tie off. Direct the threaded

tapestry needle in and out of the stem's end two or three times, creating a slight ball. Secure all loose ends. If you're adding decorative vein lines that need to be applied before felting (see Adding Veins Before Felting, pages 77–78), do it now.

Felting the Leaves

Machine felt the leaves as directed on pages 4–7. Felt them until the knit stitches disappear and they have achieved the proper measurements when laid out wet (finished sizes are listed under Felted Measurements on page 71). They will felt within two to four cycles. Once felted, tug and pull each wet leaf into the desired shape by rounding and smoothing its edges. Tug the topmost tip to create a sharp point (for the maple leaf, you'll have several of these). Squeeze and round the stem's end to be ball-like. With a pair of scissors, trim off any unwanted bumps. Let the leaves air dry completely.

Embellishing the Leaves

You can enjoy your leaves as is or add vein lines, before or after felting, as outlined below. You can use the templates in Diagram 1 for adding the veins or create your own designs.

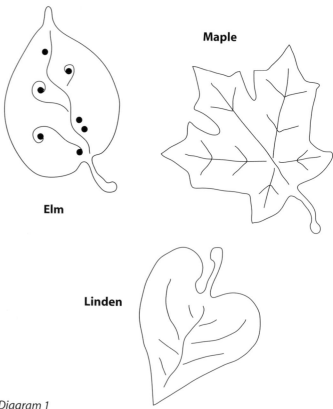

Diagram 1

ADDING VEINS BEFORE FELTING

You've got several options you can explore if you want to embellish before the leaves go into the washer.

Before you start, lightly damp press the leaf with an iron to eliminate any curling on the edges. With a quilter's pen lightly draw the veins and curly cues onto the knitted leaf. A quilter's pen (a disappearing ink marking pen) creates a visible mark as a guide on the piece so you can crochet or embroider along these lines. The design will later be washed away during the felting process. Mark the leaf enough so it can be seen and followed.

NOTE: When adding crocheted or embroidered vein lines to your knitted leaf, it is important to keep your stitches loose and even, and slightly larger than normal. If pulled too tightly, the stitches may shrink during felting and cause the leaf to pucker. Make sure the stitches lie loosely along the top of the knitted piece. Apply your stitches like you knit the initial piece: loose and sloppy!

Applied Crochet Veins

Using any size crochet hook and the same weight yarn used to knit the leaf, begin crocheting a simple chain along the pen lines. Stay loose and even!

1. Holding the yarn underneath the leaf, insert the hook from the front through the center of the first stitch you want to crochet.

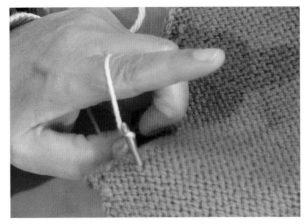

2. On the back side, yarn over the hook.

3. Pull the yarn over through the stitch to the front of the piece (1 loop on hook).

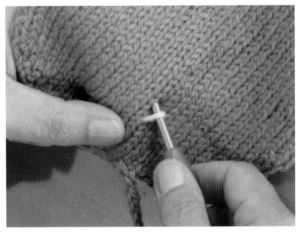

4. Insert the hook from the front through the center of the next stitch above the stitch you just went through.

5. Yarn over and pull the yarn through the stitch to the front (2 loops on hook).

6. Pull the new loop through the first (1 loop on hook).

7. Repeat Steps 4–6 until all the stitches have been worked in the desired design. Cut yarn and pull the end up and through the loop to secure it. Then thread a tapestry needle with the yarn end and direct it to the back side of the leaf to be woven in.

Embroidered Veins

You can also create veins before felting by embroidering a loose chain stitch; the effect is very similar to applied crochet veins.

Following the tutorial for the chain stitch on page 20, use a tapestry needle and the same weight yarn used to knit the leaf and embroider a loose chain stitch along the pen guidelines on the piece. Remember to keep your tension loose and even so the work won't pucker during felting. When done, secure all loose ends.

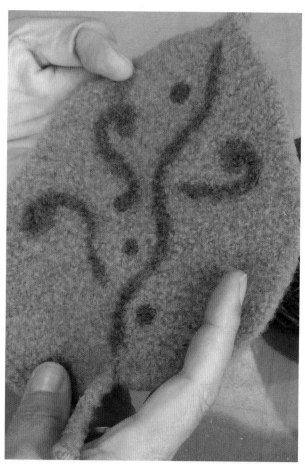

The dark green yarn contrasts against the light green leaf background. After felting, the applied crochet veins have a "knit in" look to them!

EMBELLISHMENT AFTER FELTING

For each of these options for adding embellishments, wait until the felted leaf has completely dried.

Yarn Veins and Dots

For this technique, different lengths of wool yarn are needle felted onto the leaf. You can go with a yarn color(s) that contrasts with the color of the leaf or, for a subtler effect, choose a yarn color(s) similar to that of

Experiment with vein lines using a variety of yarn colors and thicknesses. Variegated yarns make wonderful choices for the veins on these leaves; they incorporate several autumnal colors into the final design.

the leaf. Any weight wool can be used; fingering and sport weight yarns will create thin veins, worsted weight and bulky yarns create thicker ones.

Place the leaf on top of a foam pad. For the main center vein, use a long strand of yarn. For placement, refer to Diagram 1 on page 76 for each specific leaf design. With the felting needle, poke the strand into the leaf in several spots to baste it in place. Now position and baste shorter strands in place, extending out from the center vein. Shape the yarn ends into curls for a whimsical look.

When all the veins are basted into position the way you want them, poke them with the felting needle all along their length to adhere them permanently to the wool; each strand should lie firm, flat, and level with the leaf surface.

You can also add small polka dots of color to accent the vein lines, if you like. Cut several 1-inch/2.5-cm lengths of wool yarn. Pull apart the plies of each strand to create yarn fluff. Roll this fluff between your fingers to form a tiny ball. Needle felt the ball in the desired position onto the leaf.

Roving Veins

Pull loose a thin wisp of a wool roving. Gently roll the roving lengthwise between your hands, creating a tube-like strand. Position this strand lengthwise on the center of the leaf. Poke the roving with a felting needle in spots along its length to baste it down. Pull loose another thin

wisp, roll, position, and baste it. Overlap each piece slightly with the last to create one continuous line. Keep adding roving for the whole length of the leaf. Add shorter veins extending out from the main one.

You can create depth along the main vein by adding thin lines of roving in another color either on top of or next to the original vein. You can vary the width of the veins by rolling the roving gently to create wider strands or firmly for thinner strands.

When all the veins are basted into position, poke them again to adhere them permanently to the wool; the roving should lie firm, flat, and level with the leaf surface.

To finish, lightly wet the veins and a soft-bristle toothbrush with water. Gently brush the veins back and forth, adding more water if needed. The water and brushing will blend the roving with the felted wool fibers to create a smoother surface and eliminate any holes left behind by the felting needle. Lay a towel over the leaf and gently press to blot off excess water. Allow the leaf to air dry completely.

Appliqué Designs

These felted leaves lend themselves to endless wool felt appliqué designs and detailing.

To create a leaf similar to the one shown in the photo below, cut squares of wool felt and taper them to fit within the leaf's shape. The wool pieces are then adhered to the leaf using a variety of simple embroidery stitches: blanket stitch, feather stitch, and overhand stitch. See pages 20–22 for tutorials on these stitches.

Happy leaf making!

The appliqué and embroidery used on this elm leaf are quick and easy techniques. The final result is both a work of art and functional as a candle rug for your coffee table.

Harvest Pumpkins

Create your own pumpkin harvest without ever leaving the house. This autumn, felt a basketful of colorful pumpkins in various sizes and colors!

Felted Measurements

Small: 3^1/$_2$ inches/9 cm wide
Medium: 4^1/$_2$ inches/11 cm wide
Large: 5^1/$_2$ to 6 inches/14 to 15 cm wide

Materials

NOTE: When choosing yarns, do not use a machine washable yarn (like superwash merino) as it will not felt. Also, white yarns generally don't felt well. For a list of cream and other off-white yarns that do felt reliably, see page 2.

Small Pumpkin

- Color A (pumpkin): 48 yd./44 m orange 100% wool #2 sport weight yarn
- Color B (stem and leaf): 4 yd./4 m green 100% wool #2 sport weight yarn
- US 8/5.0 mm set of double-pointed needles

Medium Pumpkin

- Color A (pumpkin): 62 yd./57 m orange 100% wool #4 medium worsted weight yarn
- Color B (stem and leaf): 3 yd./3 m green 100% wool #4 medium worsted weight yarn
- US 10^1/$_2$/6.5 mm set of double-pointed needles
- US 10^1/$_2$/6.5 mm circular needles, 16 inches/41 cm long.

Large Pumpkin

- Color A (pumpkin): 62 yd./57 m orange 100% wool #4 medium worsted weight yarn (2 strands knit together for solid color pumpkin or 1 strand plus Color A1 yarn)
- Color A1 (second color for creating a variegated version): 62 yd./57 m gold 100% wool #4 medium worsted weight yarn
- Color B (stem and leaf): 6 yd./5.5 m green 100% wool #4 medium worsted weight yarn; two strands are knit together for the stem, and only one when knitting the leaf
- US 13/9 mm set of double-pointed needles
- US 13/9 mm circular needle, 16 inches/41 cm long.

All Sizes

- Stitch marker
- Tapestry needle
- Sharp tapestry needle
- Chenille needle
- Polyester fiberfill stuffing
- Cotton embroidery floss in coordinating color with pumpkin yarn, for furrow lines
- 8-inch/20-cm upholstery needle, for furrow lines
- 38-gauge all-purpose felting needle, for pumpkin blossom
- 10-inch/25-cm length of 24-gauge wire, for curly vine
- Size 6 or 8 green seed beads, any color, for curly vine
- Black acrylic felt, for pumpkin faces (optional)
- 40-gauge fine felting needle, for pumpkin faces (optional)

Notes

- For the Large pumpkin, you will knit with Color A and A1 at the same time.
- Knitting the stem and leaf in different colors is optional; the directions are for knitting them in the same color.
- Switch from dpns to the circular needle and back again as is comfortable to you.

Special Stitches

inc 1: Increase one stitch by knitting into the front and then back of same stitch.
ssk: Slip, slip, knit. Slip one stitch as if to knit onto the right needle, then slip another in the same way. Insert the left needle into the front of the two slipped stitches. Knit these stitches together; this creates a left-slanting decrease.

On preceding page: The large pumpkin was knit with Brown Sheep Nature Spun Worsted #308 Sunburst Gold and #N17 French Clay knit together, with #104 for the stem and #148 for the leaf.

Harvest Pumpkins

PUMPKIN BODY

With one strand of Color A yarn (Small and Medium sizes) or two strands Color A yarn (Large solid-color pumpkin) or one strand of each Color A and A1 yarns together (variegated Large) and the appropriate size dpns, loosely CO 12 sts. Divide sts evenly among 3 dpns, taking care not to twist them. Join to work in the rnd.

Rnd 1: *Inc 1, k1*; repeat *to* to end of rnd (18 sts). Place a stitch marker to indicate beg of rnd.
Rnd 2: Knit.
Rnd 3: *Inc 1, k2*; repeat *to* to end of rnd (24 sts).
Rnd 4: Knit.
Rnd 5: *Inc 1, k3*; repeat *to* to end of rnd (30 sts).
Rnd 6: Knit.
Rnd 7: *Inc 1, k4*; repeat *to* to end of rnd (36 sts).
Rnd 8: Knit.
Rnd 9: *Inc 1, k5*; repeat *to* to end of rnd (42 sts).
Rnd 10: Knit.
Rnd 11: *Inc 1, k6*; repeat *to* to end of rnd (48 sts).
Rnd 12: Knit.
Rnd 13: *Inc 1, k7*; repeat *to* to end of rnd (54 sts).
Rnd 14: Knit.
Rnd 15: *Inc 1, k8*; repeat *to* to end of rnd (60 sts).
Rnd 16: Knit.
Rnd 17: *Inc 1, k9*; repeat *to* to end of rnd (66 sts).
Rnds 18–32: Knit.
Rnd 33: *Ssk, k6, k2tog, k1*; repeat *to* to end of rnd (54 sts).
Rnd 34: Knit.
Rnd 35: *Ssk, k4, k2tog, k1*; repeat *to* to end of rnd (42 sts).
Rnd 36: Knit.
Rnd 37: *Ssk, k2, k2tog, k1*; repeat *to* to end of rnd (30 sts).
Rnd 38: Knit.
Rnd 39: *Ssk, k2tog, k1*; repeat *to* to end of rnd (18 sts).
Rnd 40: Knit.
Rnd 41: *K2tog, k1*; repeat *to* to end of rnd (12 sts).
Rnd 42: Knit.
Rnd 43: *K2tog*; repeat *to* to end of rnd (6 sts).
Break Color A yarn or Color A and A1 yarns, leaving a 6-inch/15-cm tail.

PUMPKIN STEM

NOTE: For the Large pumpkin, knit the stem using two strands of Color B yarn; for Small and Medium use a single strand.

Rnd 1: Join Color B yarn. Knit all 6 sts onto one dpn. Remove stitch marker. Do not turn work. Slide the work to the right of the needle.
Rnds 2–9: Knit. Do not turn work. Slide the work to the right of the needle.
Break Color B yarn, leaving 6-inch/15-cm tail. Using a tapestry needle, thread tail through last 6 sts from right to left and tie off. Secure all loose ends.

PUMPKIN LEAF

With Color B yarn and dpns, CO 5 sts.
Row 1: K1, inc 1, k1, inc 1, k1 (7 sts).
Row 2: Purl.
Row 3: K1, inc 1, k3, inc 1, k1 (9 sts).
Row 4: Purl.
Row 5: K1, inc 1, k5, inc 1, k1 (11 sts).
Row 6: Purl.
Row 7: BO 3 sts, k7 (8 sts).
Row 8: BO 3 sts kwise, p4 (5 sts).
Row 9: Knit.
Row 10: P2tog, p1, p2tog (3 sts).
Row 11: Knit.
Row 12: P3tog (1 st).
Break Color B yarn, leaving a 6-inch/15-cm tail. Thread tail through last st and tie off. Secure all loose ends.

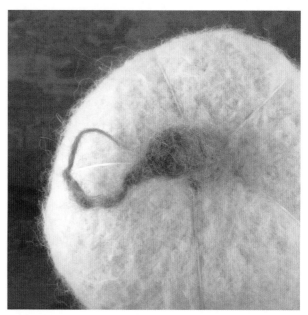

Leave the tail at the end of the stem, so the yarn will felt like a curly vine with no need to add extra detailing.

Felting the Pumpkin and the Leaf

Machine felt as directed on pages 4–7 until the knit stitches disappear. The pumpkin and leaf will felt within one to three cycles. Be sure to check the pumpkin periodically. Once felted, tug and pull the stem into desired shape, indenting the end slightly. Stuff the wet pumpkin firmly with fiberfill, rounding out its shape. Tug and pull the leaf into shape. Allow the pumpkin and leaf to air dry completely.

Once dry, close the opening at the pumpkin's bottom by sewing it shut with a chenille needle and a strand of pumpkin color yarn.

Assembling the Pumpkin

MAKING THE PUMPKIN'S FURROW LINES

Cut 1 yard/1 m of coordinating color embroidery floss. Thread the upholstery needle with all six plies of the floss. Tie a double knot at one end.

Starting at the pumpkin base, sew one to two stitches to anchor the floss and then guide the needle into the

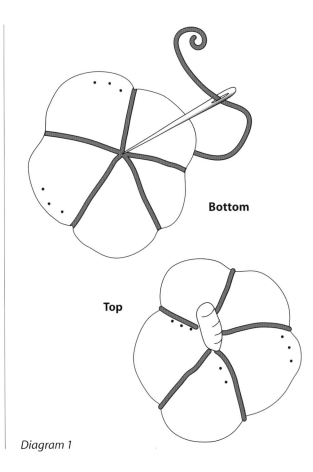

Bottom

Top

Diagram 1

A silk ribbon was used instead of a knitted pumpkin leaf and a green florist wire replaces the traditional beaded curly vine. Little green seed beads add additional texture to the pumpkin's surface.

pumpkin's center up through and out the top where the stem and the pumpkin meet. Direct the needle back down to the bottom, coming out and catching the floss, and then up through the center, this time coming out slightly to the left of the first furrow line. Pull the floss until it is taut against the pumpkin. The tighter the pull, the deeper the furrow line into the pumpkin. Direct the needle back to the bottom again.

Repeat until five to six furrow lines have been created as shown in Diagram 1. To finish, secure the end by sewing a tiny stitch or two at the pumpkin's center bottom. Bury the end within the pumpkin. The pumpkin's blossom end will cover any knots and small stitches.

NEEDLE FELTING THE PUMPKIN'S ROVING BLOSSOM END

Create a blossom end out of yarn to conceal the knot and any stitching at the pumpkin's bottom. Cut several 1-inch/ 2.5-cm pieces of Color B yarn. Pull the plies of each piece apart and rub them between your fingers to create little fluffs of yarn roving. Roll all the roving pieces together into a ball between your hands.

Place the ball over the knots and stitches. With the felting needle, poke the roving until it lays firm, flat, and smooth against the pumpkin's surface. Wet the roving with a little water. Gently rub your wet finger back and forth over the roving to smooth and eliminate any holes left behind by the felting needle.

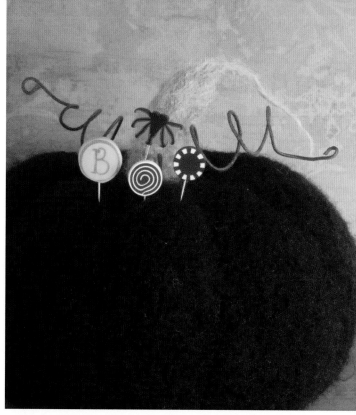

Felted pumpkins make wonderful pincushions. Add whimsical details for a special gift. This pumpkin was knit using Brown Sheep Nature Spun Worsted #601 Pepper and Berroco Ultra Alpaca #62103 Green Bean for the stem.

MAKING THE PUMPKIN'S CURLY VINE

To make the beaded vine, thread the sharp tapestry needle with a 10-inch/25-cm length of 24-gauge wire. Direct the needle through the top of the leaf's flat side about $^1/_2$ inch/1.25 cm from the edge. Now direct the needle into the base of the stem and out the other side. This will secure the leaf to the pumpkin.

Remove the wire from the needle. Adjust the wire so more of it rests on one side of the stem than the other. Begin stringing beads to within 1 inch/2.5 cm from one end. Create a tiny loop at the wire's end to prevent the beads from sliding off. Repeat for the other end of the wire.

Wrap each of the beaded wires around a pencil, forming curls. Create three or four curls on the longer side and two or three curls on the shorter one.

ADDING THE JACK-O'-LANTERN FACES

Use buttons, embroidery, and/or pieces of felt to create friendly or spooky jack-o'-lantern faces.

For felt faces, cut out shapes from black acrylic felt using the templates shown in Diagram 2 (you may want to adjust the size for smaller or larger pumpkins). With the 40-gauge fine felting needle, poke the felt pieces onto the pumpkin to adhere them flush with the wool's surface.

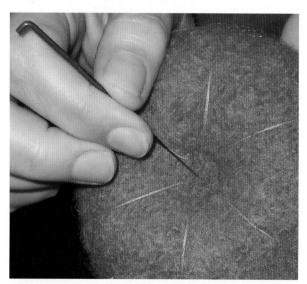

The pumpkin blossom end will cover any knots or unsightly stitches, giving your pumpkin a finished look.

Actual size

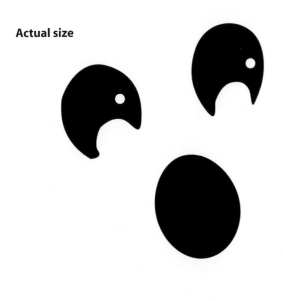

Actual size

Diagram 2

Once needle felted, wet the felt pieces with water. Wet a soft-bristle toothbrush and gently brush the felt back and forth, adding more water if needed. The water and brushing soften the felt and create a smoother surface. It also eliminates any holes left behind by the felting needle. Lay a towel over the face and gently press to blot off the excess water. Allow the pumpkin to air dry completely.

Give the eyes a little twinkle by creating a highlight dot. Sew either a yellow or white seed bead onto the black felt eyes.

Buttons help create a one-of-a-kind jack-o'-lantern pumpkin. French knots and simple straight stitches using yarns in either fingering or sport weight add further detail.

Vintage-Style
Ball Ornaments

Make an ornament for each member of your family or as a special teacher's gift. Mix and match ornament sizes (small, medium, and large) and embellishments so no two ornaments need ever be the same!

Felted Measurements

Measured from the base to the crown.
Small: 2 to 2^1/$_2$ inches/5 to 6.5 cm
Medium: 3 to 3^1/$_2$ inches/7.5 to 9 cm
Large: 4 to 4^1/$_2$ inches/10 to 11.5 cm

Materials

NOTE: When choosing yarns, do not use a machine washable yarn (like superwash merino) as it will not felt. Also, white yarns generally don't felt well. For a list of cream and other off-white yarns that do felt reliably, see page 2. The colors and brands listed are for the ornaments shown in the photo opposite.

- Color A (ornament balls):
  Small: 10 yd./9 m 100% wool #4 worsted weight yarn in any color [Frog Tree Alpaca Sport #000 Cream (2 strands were carried together to equal worsted weight), 130 yd./119 m per skein]
  Medium: 18 yd./16.5 m 100% wool #4 worsted weight yarn in any color (Brown Sheep Nature Spun Worsted #N46 Red Fox, 245 yd./225 m per skein)
  Large: 30 yd./27.5 m 100% wool #3 or #4 worsted weight yarns in any color (Cascade 220 Worsted #8903 Primavera, 220 yd./200 m per skein)
- Color B (ornament caps): 3 yd./2.75 m cream 100% wool #4 worsted weight yarn (Cascade 220 Worsted #8010 Cream, 220 yd./200 m per skein)
- US 10^1/$_2$/6.5 mm set of double-pointed needles
- Split-ring stitch marker
- Tapestry needle
- Polyester fiberfill
- Chenille needle
- T-pins (available in fabric stores)
- 18-gauge wire, any color, for wire hook ornaments
- Wire cutter
- Needle-nose pliers
- 10 mm jump-rings (available in bead/craft store)
- Decorative holiday ornament hooks, for jump-ring ornament (available in craft/retail store)

Notes

- Each ornament is knit from the base up. An open-ended tube is created at the neck to allow ample room for stuffing the felted ornament with fiberfill. A separate cap is knit, hand felted, and sewn to the ornament's neck. The ornament is then ready for embellishing and a hook.

Special Stitches

inc 1: Increase one stitch by knitting into the front and then back of same stitch.
ssk: Slip, slip, knit. Slip one stitch as if to knit onto the right needle, then slip another in the same way. Insert the left needle into the front of the two slipped stitches. Knit these stitches together; this creates a left-slanting decrease.

The three sizes of the ball ornaments: small, medium, and large. The solid background is a perfect backdrop for a little whimsical embellishing!

Small Ornament

With Color A yarn, loosely CO 6 sts. Do not turn work. Slide work to right end of needle.

Row 1: *Inc 1*; repeat *to* to end (12 sts).
Rnd 2: Divide sts evenly among 3 dpns, taking care not to twist them. Join to work in the rnd. Knit. Place a stitch marker to indicate beg of rnd.
Rnd 3: *Inc 1, k1*; repeat *to* to end of rnd (18 sts).
Rnd 4: Knit.
Rnd 5: *Inc 1, k2*; repeat *to* to end of rnd (24 sts).
Rnds 6–10: Knit.
Rnd 11: *K2, k2tog*; repeat *to* to end of rnd (18 sts).
Rnd 12: *K1, ssk*; repeat *to* to end of rnd (12 sts).
Rnd 13: Knit.
Rnd 14: *K1, k2tog*; repeat *to* to end of rnd (8 sts).
Rnd 15: Knit all sts onto 1 dpn, turn work.
Row 16: Purl.

BO all stitches. Break Color A yarn, leaving a 6-inch/15-cm tail, and tie off. Secure the hole at the ornament's base and all loose ends.

Medium Ornament

With Color A yarn, loosely CO 6 sts. Do not turn work. Slide the work to the right of the needle.

Row 1: *Inc 1*; repeat *to* to end (12 sts).
Rnd 2: Divide sts evenly among 3 dpns, taking care not to twist them. Join to work in the rnd. Knit. Place a stitch marker to indicate beg of rnd.
Rnd 3: *Inc 1, k1*; repeat *to* to end of rnd (18 sts).
Rnd 4: Knit.
Rnd 5: *Inc 1, k2*; repeat *to* to end of rnd (24 sts).
Rnd 6: Knit.
Rnd 7: *Inc 1, k3*; repeat *to* to end of rnd (30 sts).
Rnd 8: Knit.
Rnd 9: *Inc 1, k4*; repeat *to* to end of rnd (36 sts).
Rnds 10–14: Knit.
Rnd 15: *K4, k2tog*; repeat *to* to end of rnd (30 sts).
Rnd 16: *K3, ssk*; repeat *to* to end of rnd (24 sts).
Rnd 17: *K2, k2tog*; repeat *to* to end of rnd (18 sts).
Rnd 18: *K1, ssk*; repeat *to* to end of rnd (12 sts).
Rnd 19: Knit.
Rnd 20: *K1, k2tog*; repeat *to* to end of rnd (8 sts).
Rnd 21: Knit all sts onto 1 dpn, then turn work.
Row 22: Purl.

BO all stitches. Break Color A yarn, leaving a 6-inch/15-cm tail, and tie off. Secure the hole at the ornament's base and all loose ends.

Large Ornament

With Color A yarn, loosely CO 6 sts. Do not turn work. Slide the work to the right of the needle.

Row 1: *Inc 1*; repeat *to* to end (12 sts).
Rnd 2: Divide sts evenly among 3 dpns, taking care not to twist them. Join to work in the rnd. Knit. Place a stitch marker to indicate beg of rnd.
Rnd 3: *Inc 1, k1*; repeat *to* to end of rnd (18 sts).
Rnd 4: Knit.
Rnd 5: *Inc 1, k2*; repeat *to* to end of rnd (24 sts).
Rnd 6: Knit.
Rnd 7: *Inc 1, k3*; repeat *to* to end of rnd (30 sts).
Rnd 8: Knit.
Rnd 9: *Inc 1, k4*; repeat *to* to end of rnd (36 sts).
Rnd 10: Knit.
Rnd 11: *Inc 1, k5*; repeat *to* to end of rnd (42 sts).
Rnd 12: Knit.
Rnd 13: *Inc 1, k6*; repeat *to* to end of rnd (48 sts).
Rnds 14–18: Knit.
Rnd 19: *K6, k2tog*; repeat *to* to end of rnd (42 sts).
Rnd 20: *K5, ssk*; repeat *to* to end of rnd (36 sts).
Rnd 21: *K4, k2tog*; repeat *to* to end of rnd (30 sts).
Rnd 22: *K3, ssk*; repeat *to* to end of rnd (24 sts).
Rnd 23: *K2, k2tog*; repeat *to* to end of rnd (18 sts)
Rnd 24: *K1, ssk*; repeat *to* to end of rnd (12 sts).
Rnd 25: Knit.
Rnd 26: *K1, k2tog*; repeat *to* to end of rnd (8 sts).
Rnd 27: Knit all sts onto 1 dpn, then turn work.
Row 28: Purl.

BO all stitches. Break Color A yarn, leaving a 6-inch/15-cm tail, and tie off. Secure the hole at the ornament's base and all loose ends.

Felting the Ornaments

Machine felt the ornaments as directed on pages 4–7, checking on them periodically to make sure they don't felt shut and shifting the fabric slightly so it doesn't felt with a crease down the side. Felt the ornaments until the knit stitches disappear and they have achieved the proper measurements (page 87) when laid out flat wet. They will felt within two to four machine cycles. Once felted, tug and pull at the felted fabric to round out the shape.

Store-bought hooks come in a variety of shapes, sizes, and color choices. Each one adds a unique and final touch to your ornament, perfect for hanging on a tree or wreath.

Stuffing the Ornaments

While it is still wet, firmly stuff the ornament with polyester or wool fiberfill until firm and round. With a strand of ornament yarn and a chenille needle, sew the V-shaped opening at the neck's edge closed to the very top. This creates a tube at the ornament's neck with a small opening. The cap hanger will rest on this. Allow the ornament to air dry completely.

Making the Ornament Cap

This cap will fit all three size ornaments. You will adjust its
    size to fit each ornament through the hand felting
    process.
With Color B yarn, CO 12 sts.
Row 1: K1, *p2, k2*; repeat *to* to last 3 sts, p2, k1.
Row 2: P1, *k2, p2*; repeat *to* to last 3 sts, k2, p1.
Row 3: K1, *p2, k2*; repeat *to* to last 3 sts, p2, k1.
Row 4: P1, *k2, p2*; repeat *to* to last 3 sts, k2, p1.
Row 5: *P2tog*; repeat *to* to end (6 sts).
Break Color B yarn, leaving a 10-inch/25-cm tail. Using a
    tapestry needle, thread the tail through the remaining
    6 sts, from right to left, and tie off to make a ring.
    Loosely sew up the two sides, joining the cap in the
    round. Secure all loose ends.
Hand felt the cap as directed on page 7. You want to felt
    each cap so that it snugly fits the neck of the ornament
    it's being made for, so have your ornament handy,
    trying it on for size. You really want a perfect fit. The
    wet felted cap has some flexibility to be tugged to size.

Once the wet cap fits the ornament, place it on the end of your middle finger. Stretch and shape the cap to be box-like. Place the cap on the ornament to fit over the tube and press a T-pin into the cap's center to hold it tightly to the ornament. This flattens and keeps the top of the cap in position while it dries. Allow the cap to air dry completely in this position.

CREATING WIRE HOOKS AND JUMP-RING HANGERS FOR THE CAPS

There are two options for hanging the ornaments: wire hooks or jump-ring hangers. The jump-ring hanger requires attaching a second decorative hook so it can be hung on your tree. These hooks can be purchased from retail stores selling holiday decorations and come in a variety of colors and whimsical designs.

Wire Hooks

Once the cap is dry, cut a 6-inch/15-cm length of 20-gauge wire. Wrap the first inch/2.5 cm of the wire twice around a US size 10^1/$_2$/6.5 mm double-pointed needle, creating a small coil. Insert the uncoiled end up through the center of the cap's underside. Flatten the coil against the inside of the cap.

Using matching cap yarn and a chenille needle, sew a few stitches to the cap's underside, securing the coil to the wool.

With needle-nose pliers, bend the wire's end into a small curl. Then bend the entire wire around a ^{1}/$_2$- to 1-inch/1.25- to 2.5-cm wide tube or cylinder to form a half circle. Hold the curl with the pliers and slowly bend the wire into a spiral, as shown in Diagram 1. With the pliers, just up from the cap, bend the wire to the left, creating a right angle, as shown in Diagram 2.

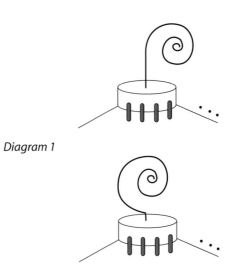

Diagram 1

Diagram 2

Jump-Ring Hangers

Once the cap is dry, take a 10 mm jump-ring and open the ends about ¹/₄ inch/.5 cm apart from each other, pulling one end forward and the other backward.

Hook one end of the ring into the cap's center and catch at least a ¹/₄-inch/.5-cm piece of the wool. A tapestry needle can help create a bigger hole for the ring to slide into. Close the attached ring by pulling each end back until they meet. Rotate the ring so the ends are buried within the cap.

Note: For the jump-ring hanger ornaments to hang on your tree, store-bought hooks are needed. Slip the purchased hook onto the ornament's ring.

Instead of knitting and felting a cap, you can use the metal cap from a plastic or glass ornament sold in craft stores. Buy them when they are on sale. The caps are easy to remove and insert into your own felted ornament. Silver beads and an embroidered silver feather stitch were used for additional contrast on top of the brown striping. The yarns used for the stripes are Brown Sheep Nature Spun Worsted #N87 Victorian Pink and #N89 Roasted Coffee, and each stripe consists of two rounds each.

SEWING THE CAPS ONTO THE ORNAMENTS

Thread a chenille needle with a strand of Color B yarn and knot one end. Direct the needle up through the cap to bury the knot inside. Place the cap on the ornament. Direct the needle back into the cap (not the same hole), through the ornament, the stuffing, and out its bottom. Snip loose ends.

Thread the chenille needle with a new strand of Color A yarn and knot one end. Inside the cap, about ¹/₄ inch up from the edge, direct the needle to the outside. This

Ornament with jump-ring hanger.

The embroidered vertical lines give the cap a finished look similar to the vintage glass ornaments of old.

Ornament with wire hook hanger.

buries the knot within. Sew ¼-inch-/.5-cm-long stitches perpendicularly along the cap's edge as shown in Diagrams 1 and 2. To finish, direct the needle into the ornament and out its side. Trim the end flush with the ornament. After the cap is sewn on, to flatten the top of the cap even further, use a 38-gauge all-purpose felting needle and poke the whole top until flat and even.

Embellishing the Ornaments

Now for the fun part! Embellish the ornaments by adding your choice of the decorative detailing ideas described below or experiment with your own. Stripes are done before felting and all the other ideas are done after. See For the Love of Detail (pages 11–27) for further tutorials and photos on these techniques.

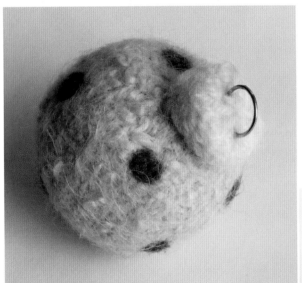

This simple small-size ornament was knit using two strands of Frog Tree Alpaca sport weight yarn to create a worsted weight. The polka dots were needle felted on after felting with a little brown roving.

This ornament's stripes are each five rounds deep. The feather stitch was embroidered where the stripes meet after the ornament was felted.

STRIPING

Knit the ornaments in stripes of green and red or, for a candy-cane effect, with red and white. Remember, for consistent felting make sure the colors are the same brand throughout the ornament. For the stripes to really show up after being felted, knit at least two rounds or more of each color. A single round of color will show up as a thin line after felting or may not even be visible, depending on the yarn color used. No need to break the yarn after each color change. Just carry the new/old color yarn up the work. Be sure to secure all loose ends and seal any holes created by adding the new yarns before felting.

NEEDLE FELTING

Use needle felting to add polka dots, curlicues, or any freestyle design of your choosing to your ornaments. For polka dots, you can needle felt small pinches of wool roving or cut out circles of acrylic or wool felt and needle felt them onto the ornament (or embroider them on for even more visual pizzazz).

BEADS, SEQUINS, AND BUTTONS

Sewing these onto an ornament adds pops of color and sparkle. You can use beads and buttons to create a variety of polka dot sizes.

EMBROIDERY

Embroidery stitches add detail and additional color to any ornament. Fingering weight yarn (doesn't have to be wool) and cotton floss can be used as embroidery threads. Embroidery is both functional in sewing felt shapes (like holly leaves or circles) to the wool as well as adding additional colors and detail to any ornament.

The holly leaves and berries were needle felted onto the ornament using little wisps of green and red wool rovings.

The robin and its nest were needle felted onto the ornament freestyle, using little scraps of roving and coordinating yarns. The feather stitch and French knots were embroidered after the nest and robin were needle felted into place.

This ornament was knit using Berroco Ultra Alpaca worsted weight yarn #6201 Winter White. The pale sequins and silver beads offer a subtle contrast against the pearly cream yarn. A strand of silver embroidery thread was added to the knitting of the ornament cap to give it a shimmery feel.

Small pieces of yarn were needle felted onto this ornament to create curlicue swirls. Seed beads were sewn on for tiny polka dots of texture.

Holiday Place Card Holders

S tart a new family tradition this holiday season by turning the small ornaments into place card holders for that special dinner party. Your guests can even take their ornament home with them as a reminder of your hospitality.

Materials

- Felted small-size felted Vintage-Style Ball Ornaments, stuffed and allowed to air dry completely as per instructions for ornaments
- Hand-felted and dried caps for Vintage-Style Ball Ornaments
- Plastic poly-pellets, for filling ornaments
- Clipiola® Italian paper clips, found online or in art supply stores
- Decorative place cards

Pull all of the stuffing out of the now-dry ornament. Fill the ornament with the poly-pellets until full and firm but still squishy. The poly-pellets will allow the ornament to sit upright on the table. Sew the ornament's neck closed. Sew a felted cap on the ornament as directed in Vintage-Style Ball Ornaments pattern (see page 90).

Now you will create a jump-ring using the paper clip. Slip the open end of the paper clip into the top of the cap's wool and out again, just enough to catch the wool. Rotate the clip until the end is buried within the cap. Insert the name card through the clip and adjust slightly.

These clips can also be used to hang the ornaments. The poly-pellets make for a heavier ornament than the fiber-filled ones for hanging.

Stick a Pin in It!

Make yourself a pincushion using any size ball ornament you choose. Once the ornament is stuffed and dried, swap out the stuffing for poly-pellets or crushed walnut shells (found online). Crushed walnut shells will sharpen your pins each time they are inserted into the ornament. If you decide to use walnut shells, place them in a muslin bag and sew the opening shut to prevent them from leaking out of the ornament over time. Whether you use poly-pellets or walnut shells, stuff the ornament so it will still stand up and not wobble over. Sew a felted cap on its neck.

Just Another Button Company has a wonderful selection of decorative holiday stickpins, available online and in upscale quilting stores.

On preceding page: *This ornament was knit using Frog Tree Alpaca Sport #046 Avocado and #041 Grass Green yarns creating stripes. After felting, it was embroidered with the feather stitch to create a vine look with red seed beads sewn on for the berries.*

Crazy Quilt
Holiday Stocking

This pattern makes a large felted stocking with a simple folded cuff that lends itself to hours of embellishing, like the crazy quilts of long ago.

Felted Measurements

7 to 8 inches/18 to 20 cm wide by 22 inches/51 to 56 cm high.

Materials

NOTE: When choosing yarns, do not use a machine washable yarn (like superwash merino) as it will not felt. Also, white yarns generally don't felt well. For a list of cream and other off-white yarns that do felt reliably, see page 2. The colors and brands listed are for the stocking shown in the photo opposite.

- Color A: 209 yd./191 m 100% wool #4 worsted weight yarn (shown in Cascade 220 Worsted #8886 Italian Plum, 220 yd./200 m per skein)
- Color B: 110 yd./101 m 100% wool #4 worsted weight yarn (shown in Cascade 220 Worsted #9430 Highland Green, 220 yd./200 m per skein)
- Color C: 143 yd./131 m 100% wool #4 worsted weight yarn (shown in Cascade 220 Worsted #9404 Ruby, 220 yd./200 m per skein)
- Color D: 73 yd./67 m 100% wool #4 worsted weight yarn (shown in Cascade 220 Worsted #8903 Primavera, 200 yd./200 m per skein)
- Color E (optional cording): 14 yd./13 m 100% wool #4 worsted weight yarn (shown in Cascade 220 Worsted #7827 Goldenrod, 220 yd./200 m per skein)
- Color F (jingle bell): 11 yd./10 m 100% wool #4 worsted weight yarn (shown in Cascade 220 Worsted #9404 Ruby Red, 220 yd./200 m per skein)
- US size 10¹/₂/6.5 mm set of double-pointed needles
- US size 10¹/₂/6.5 mm circular needles, 24 inches/61 cm long
- 2 stitch markers
- 2 split-ring stitch markers
- Tapestry needle
- Chenille needle
- 1 yd./1 m gold fingering wool yarn or embroidery floss, for jingle bell embroidered design

Optional materials for embellishment

- Embroidery floss or fingering or sport weight yarns, for embroidery
- Buttons of various colors and sizes
- Acrylic or wool felt

Notes

- The stocking is knit in rounds from the top down to the heel flap.
- The heel flap is knit in rows, then turned and attached to the stocking.
- Be very mindful to knit with a consistent, loose tension. If you tighten up as you knit the stocking, that section will felt more quickly than the top of the stocking and be narrower than you want. Stay consistently loose and sloppy! It will be huge and crazy looking.

Special Stitches

inc 1: Increase one stitch by knitting into the front and then back of same stitch.

ssk: Slip, slip, knit. Slip one stitch as if to knit onto the right needle, then slip another in the same way. Insert the left needle into the front of the two slipped stitches. Knit these stitches together; this creates a left-slanting decrease.

Crazy Quilt Holiday Stocking

STOCKING CUFF

Using Color A yarn and circular needles, loosely CO 75 sts. Being careful not to twist sts, join to work in the rnd.

Rnd 1: Purl. Place a stitch marker to indicate beg of rnd.

Rnds 2–4: Knit.

Rnd 5: *K14, inc 1*; repeat *to* to end of rnd (80 sts).

Rnds 6–45: Knit 40 rounds.

Rnd 46: At beg of rnd place a stitch marker (A) on st immediately below stitch marker at beg of rnd. Knit 40 sts and place a second stitch marker (B) on st immediately below the last stitch. Knit to end of rnd, and then turn work.

NOTE: You are now at the fold of the stocking. The stitches marked by A and B will be used later on for the Stocking Hanger Cording. The work is also turned at this point so that once the cuff is folded over it will lay knit side atop the knit side of the stocking body.

STOCKING BODY

Rnds 1–10: Knit. Break Color A yarn, leaving a 6-inch/15-cm tail.

NOTE: From this point forward, it is important to keep your tension uniformly loose (see Notes above).

Rnd 11: Join Color B yarn, knit to end of rnd.

Rnds 12–71: Knit 60 rounds. Break Color B yarn, leaving a 6-inch/15-cm tail.

Rnd 72: Join Color C yarn, knit to end of rnd.

Rnds 73–101: Knit 29 rounds.

Rnd 102: K38, k2tog, k38, k2tog (78 sts).

STOCKING HEEL

NOTE: As you work the heel flap, continue to transfer the end of rnd stitch marker from row to row.

Row 1: K19, then turn work.

Row 2: P38, break Color C yarn, leaving a 6-inch/15-cm tail, then turn work.

Row 3: Join Color A yarn, k38.

Row 4: P38.

Row 5: K38.

Row 6: P38.

Rows 7–22: Rep [Rows 5 and 6] 8 times.

Row 23: Knit.

Row 24: Purl to 3 sts past stitch marker, p2tog, p1, turn work (37 sts).

Row 25: Sl 1, knit to 3 sts past marker, k2tog, k1, turn work (36 sts).

Row 26: Sl 1, purl to 1 st before gap, sliding st marker when you come to it, p2tog, p1, turn work (1 st dec'd).

Row 27: Sl 1, knit to 1 stitch before gap, sliding st marker when you come to it, k2tog, k1, turn work (1 st dec'd).

[Repeat Rows 26 and 27] 5 times until only 1 st remains after gap on both sides (24 sts), then turn work.

Next row: Sl 1, purl to last 2 sts, p2tog (23 sts), then turn work.

Next row: Sl 1, knit to last 2 sts, k2tog (22 sts).

FOOT OF STOCKING

With right circular needle, pick up 12 sts along left side of heel flap and join to begin knitting in the rnd again. Place a stitch marker at this point. Break Color A yarn, leaving a 6-inch/15-cm tail.

Join Color C yarn, k12, k2tog, k12, k2tog, k12. Place a second stitch marker. Pick up 12 sts along right side of heel flap. Knit 11 sts to beg of rnd (84 sts).

Rnd 1: Knit.

Rnd 2: Knit to 3 sts before first marker, ssk, k1, slide marker, k38, slide second marker, k1, ssk, knit to end of rnd (2 sts dec'd).

Rnd 3: Knit.

Rnd 4: Knit to 3 sts before first marker, k2tog, k1, slide marker, k38, slide second marker, k1, k2tog, knit to end of rnd (2 sts dec'd).

Rnd 5: Knit.

[Repeat Rnds 2–5] 3 times (68 sts).

Next rnd: Knit to 3 sts before first marker, ssk, k1, remove first marker, k38, remove second marker, k1, ssk, knit to end (66 sts).

Next rnd: Knit. Break Color C yarn, leaving a 6-inch/15-cm tail.

STOCKING TOE

Join Color D yarn.

Rnds 1–25: Knit 25 rounds. Break Color D yarn, leaving a 6-inch/15-cm tail.

NOTE: Switch to dpns at any time to make knitting in the rnd easier.

Rnd 26: Join Color B yarn, *k9, ssk*; repeat *to* to end of rnd (60 sts).

Rnds 27–28: Knit.

Rnd 29: *K8, k2tog*; repeat *to* to end of rnd (54 sts).

Rnds 30–31: Knit.

Rnd 32: *K7, ssk*; repeat *to* to end of rnd (48 sts).

Rnds 33–34: Knit.

Rnd 35: *K6, k2tog*; repeat *to* to end of rnd (42 sts).

Rnd 36: Knit.

Rnd 37: *K5, ssk*; repeat *to* to end of rnd (36 sts).

Rnd 38: Knit.

Rnd 39: *K4, k2tog*; repeat *to* to end of rnd (30 sts).

Rnd 40: Knit.

Rnd 41: *K3, ssk*; repeat *to* to end of rnd (24 sts).

Rnd 42: Knit.

Rnd 43: *K2, k2tog*; repeat *to* to end of rnd (18 sts).

Rnd 44: Knit.

Rnd 45: *K1, ssk*; repeat *to* until end (12 sts).

Break Color B yarn, leaving a 6-inch/15-cm tail. Using a tapestry needle, thread tail through the last 12 sts and tie off. Secure all holes and loose ends.

STOCKING HANGER CORDING

Fold the stocking's cuff over and locate the two stitch markers (A and B) as shown in Diagram 1.

At the fold where the purl and knit stitches meet, at stitch marker B, use the circular needle to pick up the lower loop of each purl stitch, moving clockwise, for a total of 80 sts. Do not pick up more than 80 sts (1 or 2 sts less than 80 is fine).

With two dpns and Color D yarn, CO 3 sts and begin knitting the I-cord bind-off as follows: Slide the 3 sts from the dpn onto the tip of the left circular needle. With the dpn, knit the first 2 sts off, and slip the next stitch as if to knit. Knit another stitch from the circular needle. Pass the slipped stitch over the previously knitted stitch and off the needle. Slide these 3 sts from the dpn back onto the circular needle and repeat this process until marker A is reached, leaving the sts on the dpn instead of transferring them back to the circular needle. With two dpns, use the 3 sts to knit an I-cord 5 inches/13 cm long separate from the stocking edge. This is the hanger loop and should be on the heel side of the stocking!

At 5 inches/13 cm, slide the 3 sts from the dpn back onto the left circular needle. Repeat the I-cord bind-off, joining the hanger loop to the stocking edge. When you reach marker B, and with 3 sts left on the dpn, break Color D yarn, leaving a 6-inch/15-cm tail. Using the tapestry needle, thread the tail through the 3 sts, from right to left, and tie off. Sew both cord ends to the stocking and one another, overlapping them slightly so they appear as one continuous cord. Secure all loose ends.

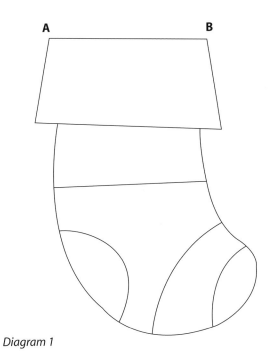

Diagram 1

Making the Optional Stocking Edge Cording

Knitting an I-cord along the cuff's edge adds another accent color to the stocking.

Turn the stocking so the toe is facing up and to the left. With the circular needle, moving clockwise, pick up the lower loops of the topmost purl stitches all around the cuff's edge until you have 75 sts.

With two dpns and Color E yarn, CO 3 sts. Do not turn work. Begin knitting the I-cord bind-off as follows: Slide the 3 sts from the dpn onto the tip of left circular needle.

The edge cording adds additional color to your stocking. Choose a color for your cording from one of the several embroidery colors intended to adorn your stocking; this will help to create continuity throughout the stocking.

With the dpn, knit the first 2 sts off the needle. Slip the next stitch as if to knit. Knit another stitch from the circular needle. Pass the slipped stitch over the previously knitted stitch and off the needle. Slide these 3 sts from the dpn back to the circular needle. Repeat the process again until you have bound off all the sts on the circular needle and have 3 sts left on the dpn.

Break Color E yarn, leaving a 6-inch/15-cm tail. Using a tapestry needle, thread the tail through the remaining 3 sts, from right to left, and tie off. Sew both the I-cord ends to the stocking and one another, overlapping them slightly so they appear as one continuous cord. Secure all loose ends.

Felting the Stocking

Machine felt the stocking as directed on pages 4–7 until the knit stitches disappear and the wet stocking laid out flat measures 7 to 8 inches/18 to 20 cm wide by 20 to 22/51 to 56 cm inches high. It will take one to three cycles to felt. Be sure to check on the stocking periodically, opening it up so it doesn't felt shut and to prevent permanent creases from forming.

Once felted, tug and pull the stocking into the desired shape. To prevent the stocking from drying absolutely flat, stuff it with paper towels or plastic bags to round out its shape. Let the stocking air dry completely on a sweater rack, occasionally turning it over.

Embellishing the Stocking

There is a world of opportunity here, and you should spend time in the chapter For the Love of Detail for tutorials and ideas. But as far as I'm concerned, a Crazy Quilt

Hearts and circles were blanket stitched onto the stocking using fingering weight yarns. Buttons and felted bobbles create colorful accents. Experiment with a variety of embroidery stitches.

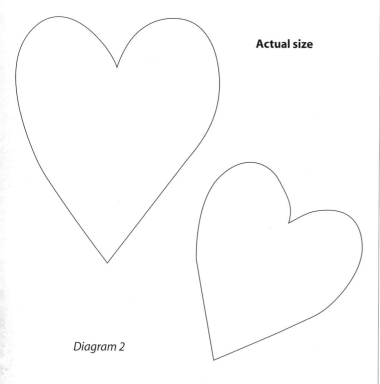

Actual size

Diagram 2

Stocking is all about embroidery. The four basic stitches I use the most are the French knot, chain stitch, feather stitch, and blanket stitch. Any fingering weight yarn and/or cotton embroidery floss will work well. Mix the French knots with the feather stitch to create a wandering vine with berries, or create stripes with the chain stitch. Where two blocks of color meet, embroider the blanket stitch to add another accent color.

You can also embroider on appliqué shapes like the hearts shown above. Trace and cut the heart templates in Diagram 2 from any color wool felt, then position and embroider them onto the stocking using the blanket or

the overhand stitch along their edges. Feel free to sew on beads or use additional decorative stitching.

Finally, you can knit and felt a jingle bell to sew onto your stocking's toe.

Jingle Bell

With Color F yarn and two dpns, CO 3 sts, leaving a 10-inch/25-cm tail.
Row 1 (RS): *Inc 1*; repeat *to* to the end (6 sts).
Row 2 (WS): Purl.
Row 3: *Inc 1*; repeat *to* to the end (12 sts).
Row 4: Purl.
Row 5: *Inc 1, k1*; repeat *to* to the end (18 sts).
Row 6: Purl.
Row 7: *K2tog, k1*; repeat *to* to the end (12 sts).
Row 8: Purl.
Row 9: *K2tog*; repeat *to* to the end (6 sts).
Row 10: Purl.
Row 11: *K2tog*; repeat *to* to the end (3 sts).
BO all sts. Break Color F yarn, leaving a 2-yd./2-m long tail.

Using a tapestry needle, thread the tail. Fold the piece in half, right side out and sides touching, then loosely sew up the side, leaving a small opening at the other end. Squish all of the yarn tail into the ball. Sew the opening closed. Secure all loose ends.

With hot running water from the kitchen faucet and a little hand soap, wet the knitted ball. Alternate between rolling the ball vigorously between your palms and running it under hot water, adding more soap when needed. Hand felt the ball until it is firm, round, and about 1 inch/2.5 cm in diameter. Rinse the ball under cold water to get the soap out. Blot dry between towels. Roll the felted ball between your palms to further shape it. Allow the ball to air dry completely.

NOTE: If making more than one jingle bell, machine felt them for a cycle or two, then finish felting and shaping them by hand under hot running water. This saves on the wear-and-tear of your hands!

Once dry, embroider the jingle bell design shown below. Use gold fingering weight yarn or embroidery floss and a chenille needle to stitch two straight lines and four French knots on one end of the ball. Attach the jingle bell by sewing it onto the stocking's toe using matching stocking yarn and the chenille needle. Bury the loose end within the stocking.

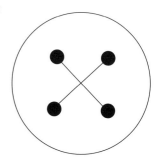

Jingle Bell embroidery design.

Woolly
Snowman

S tay inside by the crackling fire and knit yourself a pint-size snowman. No matter how cold or snowy it is, this charming fellow will warm any heart. Knitting woolly snowmen may never replace rolling your own outside, but it comes woolly darn close!

Even better, with just a few adjustments, this basic snowman pattern can be knit and felted into a stack of three pumpkins with whimsical black felt faces or a Santa snowman complete with toy bag and stocking cap!

Felted Measurements

Felted and filled with poly-pellets, the snowman will stand about 8^{1}/$_{2}$ inches/22 cm tall without his hat.

Materials

NOTE: When choosing yarns, do not use a machine washable yarn (like superwash merino) as it will not felt. Also, white yarns generally don't felt well. For a list of cream and other off-white yarns that do felt reliably, see page 2. The colors and brands listed are for the snowman shown on preceding page.

- Color A (snowman): 106 yd./97 m cream 100% wool #4 worsted weight yarn (shown in Patons Classic Wool Worsted #202 Aran, 210 yd./192 m per skein)
- Color B (top hat): 20 yd./18 m black 100% wool #4 worsted weight yarn (shown in Patons Classic Wool Worsted #226 Black, 210 yd./192 m per skein)
- Color C (scarf): 18 yd./16.5 m red 100% wool #4 worsted weight yarn (shown in Patons Classic Wool Worsted #230 Bright Red, 210 yd./192 m per skein)
- US size 10^{1}/$_{2}$/6.5 mm set of double-pointed needles
- US size 10^{1}/$_{2}$/6.5 mm circular needles, 16 inches/ 40.5 cm long
- Split-ring stitch marker
- Tapestry needle
- 2 or 3 small black buttons
- Chenille needle
- Polyester fiberfill
- Plastic poly-pellets
- Red and green sport weight yarn or embroidery floss, for holly and berries stitching on top hat (optional)
- Orange oven-bake clay, for clay carrot (I find Sculpey® brand is soft and easy to sculpt with; one brick of clay will make about 60 carrots)
- Sharp-ended toothpicks, for clay carrot and corncob pipe
- ^{1}/$_{2}$ x ^{3}/$_{4}$-inch/1.25 x 2-cm cork stopper, for concob pipe
- Small tube of E-6000 craft glue, for clay carrot
- Orange 100% wool roving, for roving carrot
- 38-gauge all-purpose felting needle, for roving carrot

- Foam pad, for roving carrot nose
- Black size 6 seed beads, for arms
- Black 24-gauge bead wire, for arms
- Wire cutter, for arms
- Needle-nose pliers, for arms
- ^{1}/$_{4}$-inch-/.5 cm-wide black grosgrain or satin ribbon, for hat band (optional)
- ^{1}/$_{2}$ x ^{3}/$_{4}$-inch/1.25 x 2-cm cork stopper, for corncob pipe
- 1-inch/2.5-cm unpainted wooden flowerpot, found in craft store, for potted tree
- Sprig of silk evergreen branch, for potted tree
- Hot glue gun and glue, for potted tree
- Acrylic paint, any color, for potted tree
- Beads of various sizes, for strand of garland around potted tree

Notes

- Woolly Snowman (and his variations) is knit from the bottom up in the round.
- His top hat and scarf are knit separately.
- As you knit the snowballs, the stitch count increases and then decreases. Switch back and forth between the dpns and circular needle to make knitting in the round more comfortable for you.
- You can make the snowman's nose from oven-bake clay or wool roving. Directions are provided for both.
- Black buttons have been specified for the snowman, but you can experiment with colored buttons, brads, and charms. Vary the sizes, layering them one atop the other.

Special Stitches

inc 1: Increase one stitch by knitting into the front and then back of same stitch.
k2togTBL: Knit two stitches together through their back loops; this creates a left-slanting decrease.

Woolly Snowman

BOTTOM SNOWBALL

With Color A yarn and dpns, loosely CO 12 sts. Divide the sts evenly among 3 dpns, taking care not to twist them. Join to work in the rnd.

Rnd 1: *Inc 1, k1*; repeat *to* to end of rnd (18 sts). Place a stitch marker to indicate beg of rnd.
Rnd 2: Knit.
Rnd 3: *Inc 1, k2*; repeat *to* to end of rnd (24 sts).
Rnd 4: Knit.
Rnd 5: *Inc 1, k3*; repeat *to* to end of rnd (30 sts).
Rnd 6: Knit.
Rnd 7: *Inc 1, k4*; repeat *to* to end of rnd (36 sts).
Rnd 8: Knit.
Rnd 9: *Inc 1, k5*; repeat *to* to end of rnd (42 sts).
Rnd 10: Change to circular needle, knit.
Rnd 11: *Inc 1, k6*; repeat *to* to end of rnd (48 sts).
Rnd 12: Knit.
Rnd 13: *Inc 1, k7*; repeat *to* to end of rnd (54 sts).
Rnd 14: Knit.
Rnd 15: *Inc 1, k8*; repeat *to* to end of rnd (60 sts).
Rnd 16: Knit.
Rnd 17: *Inc 1, k9*; repeat *to* to end of rnd (66 sts).
Rnd 18–32: Knit.
Rnd 33: *K9, k2tog*; repeat *to* to end of rnd (60 sts).
Rnd 34: Knit.
Rnd 35: *K8, k2togTBL*; repeat *to* to end of rnd (54 sts).
Rnd 36: *K7, k2tog*; repeat *to* to end of rnd (48 sts).
Rnd 37: *K6, k2togTBL*; repeat *to* to end of rnd (42 sts).
Rnd 38: *K5, k2tog*; repeat *to* to end of rnd (36 sts).
Rnd 39: *K4, k2togTBL*; repeat *to* to end of rnd (30 sts).
Rnd 40: Knit.

MIDDLE SNOWBALL

Rnd 1: *Inc 1, k4*; repeat *to* to end of rnd (36 sts).
Rnd 2: Knit.
Rnd 3: *Inc 1, k5*; repeat *to* to end of rnd (42 sts).
Rnd 4: Knit.
Rnd 5: *Inc 1, k6*; repeat *to* to end of rnd (48 sts).
Rnd 6: Knit.
Rnd 7: *Inc 1, k7*; repeat *to* to end of rnd (54 sts).
Rnds 8–12: Knit.
Rnd 13: *K7, k2tog*; repeat *to* to end of rnd (48 sts).
Rnd 14: Knit.
Rnd 15: *K6, k2togTBL*; repeat *to* to end of rnd (42 sts).
Rnd 16: *K5, k2tog*; repeat *to* to end of rnd (36 sts).
Rnd 17: *K4, k2togTBL*; repeat *to* to end of rnd (30 sts).
Rnd 18: *K3, k2tog*; repeat *to* to end of rnd (24 sts).
Rnd 19: Knit.

Add a Little Sparkle

Want to add a hint of sparkle to your woolly snowman, giving the felted wool a glistening snow-like effect? All you need is 100% wool white/cream worsted weight yarn and a spool of blending filament, which is a metallic, tinsel-like thread (you can find it in embroidery, fabric, or quilt stores). Either a metallic silver or gold color thread will work.

When you knit the snowman, knit the filament along with the yarn. Machine felt the snowman accordingly and then enjoy the sparkly effect. Experiment adding this filament to other projects, like the Vintage-Style Ball Ornaments.

Adding a strand of a blending filament thread such as one of these along with the worsted cream yarn creates a hint of sparkle in the felted wool.

TOP SNOWBALL

Rnd 1: Knit.
Rnd 2: *Inc 1, k3*; repeat *to* to end of rnd (30 sts).
Rnd 3: Knit.
Rnd 4: *Inc 1, k4*; repeat *to* to end of rnd (36 sts).
Rnds 5–14: Knit.
Rnd 15: *K4, k2tog*; repeat *to* to end of rnd (30 sts).
Rnd 16: Knit.
Rnd 17: *K3, K2togTBL*; repeat *to* to end of rnd (24 sts).
Rnd 18: *K2, k2tog*; repeat *to* to end of rnd (18 sts).
Rnd 19: *K1, k2togTBL*; repeat *to* to end of rnd (12 sts).
Rnd 20: Knit.
Rnd 21: *K2tog*; repeat *to* to end of rnd (6 sts).

(continued)

Break Color A yarn, leaving a 6-inch/15-cm tail. Using a tapestry needle, thread the tail through the remaining 6 sts and tie off. Secure all loose ends. Leave the opening at the snowman's base unsewn. This will allow access to stuff the snowman with fiberfill after felting.

Felting Snowman

The snowman should be machine felted separately from his hat and scarf to prevent bleeding onto the cream yarn. Shout® Color Catchers® will not prevent all bleeding, so play it safe and felt colors separately, unless you want a pink snowman. Machine felt the snowman as directed on pages 4–7 until the knit stitches disappear and the snowman laid out flat measures about 9¹⁄₂ to 10 inches/24 to 25 cm. It is important to felt your snowman to the above dimensions to ensure the felted hat and scarf will fit your finished snowman. It will take two to four cycles to felt the snowman. During the felting process, check on your snowman periodically, inserting your finger in the bottom opening to keep it from felting shut. Each time take the snowman out of the mesh bag and open up the body so it doesn't felt too flat. This prevents permanent ridges and seaming. If the opening felts too small to get your fingers into it, you can really stretch the opening to widen it. If needed, with a pair of scissors cut the opening slightly wider until it measures about 1¹⁄₂ inches/4 cm.

Assembling Snowman

Once felted, firmly stuff the wet snowman with fiberfill so that each of his snowballs is well defined. For his hat to fit, stuff the top snowball only until it measures about 7¹⁄₂ inches/19 cm around the head. Allow the snowman to air dry completely.

ADDING THE BUTTONS

Once dry, pull the fiberfill out of the bottom and middle snowballs. Thread a chenille needle with a strand of Color B yarn and knot one end. Bury the knotted end on the inside of the snowman and then sew two or three black buttons onto the middle snowball. Secure the yarn by sewing two tiny stitches on the inside wall.

ADDING THE TWIG-LIKE ARMS

To create bendable arms, cut one 15-inch/38-cm length of 24-gauge wire and fold it in half. Slide five beads onto the left side of the wire. Slide the first bead (the anchor bead) so it is close to the fold as shown in Diagram 1. Hold the other four beads between your fingers and

thread the end of the right wire through the four beads. Use needle-nose pliers to pull the threaded wire until snug around the anchor bead. This completes one finger, as shown in Diagram 2.

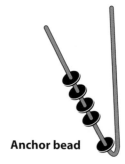

Diagram 1

Diagram 2

Slide another four beads onto the right-side wire. Slide the bead nearest the wire's end (the anchor bead) slightly to the right. With the end of the wire, bypass the anchor bead and thread the wire through the other beads. Hold the other three beads plus the first beaded finger between your fingers and, using the needle-nose pliers, pull the wire away from you until it lies snug around the anchor bead. Finger two is complete.

On the wire left of the first finger, slide another four beads onto the wire and repeat the process for the third finger. A complete hand with three fingers is shown in Diagram 3.

To finish the arm, thread more beads onto both wire ends for a total of twenty beads. Push firmly on the first

Diagram 3

couple of beads to slightly close the gap between the three fingers. Set the first arm aside. Repeat instructions and make a second arm with fingers.

To attach each arm, poke the ends of each wire into the snowman's middle until they are about $1/8$ inch/.5 cm apart from each other. Exact positioning of the arms is up to you. Inside the snowman, twist the two ends of one arm together against the inside wall. Twist all the way up the wire's length to create one thick wire. Attach the second arm to the other side of the snowman in the same way.

At the snowman's interior middle, crisscross the two wires to form an X. Adjust the internal wires so the beaded arms on the outside don't indent the felted wool. Once the arms are in position, wrap the two wires around one another to create one continuous wire connecting the arms together. Use a wire cutter to trim any sharp ends.

Don't worry if the arms seem floppy. Restuffing the snowman's middle with fiberfill will firm them up.

RESTUFFING SNOWMAN

Firmly restuff the middle snowball and upper portion of the bottom snowball with fiberfill. Begin spooning poly-pellets into the base until it is firm but still squishy. The poly-pellets create a more flexible base so that your snowman will stand better. Occasionally insert your finger into the opening to push the pellets down, creating room for more pellets. Once the base is full, place a small piece of the fiberfill just inside the opening as a plug. This will keep the poly-pellets from spilling out as the opening is sewn closed.

To close the opening, thread a chenille needle with a strand of Color A yarn. Knot one end. Sew a running stitch along the outside edge of the opening as shown in Diagram 4.

Gently pull the attached yarn to cinch shut the opening, being careful not to break the yarn. Sew several little stitches to seal the hole completely shut. Bury the loose end within the snowman.

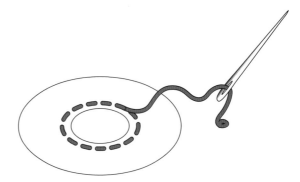

Diagram 4

ADDING THE CARROT NOSE

You can make the snowman's nose with either oven-bake clay or wool roving. A clay nose gives the snowman a different texture from all the wool, plus it holds its shape for years. The wool roving nose is in keeping with the all-wool theme and it takes just minutes to make.

Clay Carrot Nose

Preheat the oven to 275 degrees F/135 degrees C. Pull off a small piece of clay. Soften the clay between your fingers by squishing it onto itself. Gently roll it into a cylinder, tapering it slightly at one end. This forms the tip of the carrot. Measure and trim the carrot's thicker end with a knife so it is about $7/8$ inch/2.25 cm long.

Gently roll the carrot's tip area again to make it pointier. The finished carrot should measure about 1 inch/2.5 cm long. Poke a sharp toothpick about halfway into the carrot's broader side. Using a knife, press the clay slightly around the toothpick, but keep its base flat. Make several carrots in this way, and then place them on a baking sheet, making sure they don't touch each other. Bake them for fifteen minutes. Remove the pan from the oven and let the baked carrots cool completely.

Once cooled, if the toothpick didn't stick to the clay, apply a small amount of glue to the toothpick and reinsert it into the carrot. Wipe away any excess glue and allow it to dry completely.

To position the carrot, poke it into the center of the snowman's face, right up from the buttons. Ease the carrot out from the wool about 1 inch/2.5 cm. With another toothpick, carefully apply glue to the toothpick between the carrot and the wool's surface, and to the backside of the carrot. Apply the glue sparingly to prevent pooling and clumping. Press the carrot against the snowman's face. Twist the carrot slightly so it lies firm

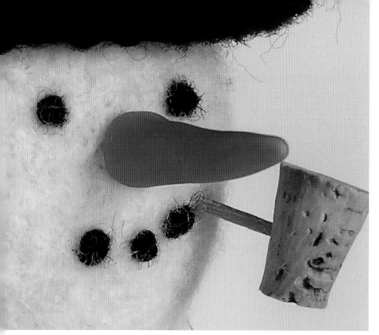

Woolly Snowman proudly displays his newly placed clay carrot for a nose.

and not indented against the wool. Allow the glue to dry for about an hour. The glue's strong smell will dissipate as it dries.

Once dry, squeeze the snowman's head, front to back, until the sharp toothpick end pops out the back. Break off this end.

Wool Roving Carrot Nose

Pull off a small amount of orange roving and gently roll it into a cylinder between your hands. Fold it in half and roll again. Fold and roll again. Using a felting needle, poke the roving on a foam pad, rotating it constantly so it remains three-dimensional and attains a carrot shape. Using your finger to put a little more pressure on one end, gently roll the carrot into the palm of your hand to create a point. The finished carrot should measure about 1 1/4 inches/3 cm long. If the carrot is too long, trim its broad end to size with the scissors. If too short, gently roll the carrot again to lengthen it slightly.

To position the carrot, center it on the snowman's face, right up from the buttons. With the felting needle, poke the carrot's outer edges, securing it to the head. The carrot will shorten slightly the more you poke. Continue needle felting until the carrot is secure and won't tug off. To create a pointier tip, wet your fingers and gently twist the end of the carrot. Trim any excess.

MAKING SNOWMAN'S TOP HAT

With Color B yarn and dpns, CO 30 sts. Divide the sts evenly among 3 dpns, taking care not to twist them. Join to work in the rnd.

Rnds 1–4: Knit.
Rnd 5: *K3, ssk*; repeat from *to* to end of rnd (24 sts).
Rnds 6–15: Knit.
Rnd 16: *K2, k2tog*; repeat from *to* to end of rnd (18 sts).
Rnd 17: *K1, ssk*; repeat from *to* to end of rnd (12 sts).
Rnd 18: *K2tog*; repeat from *to* to end of rnd (6 sts).
Break Color B yarn, leaving a 6-inch/15-cm tail. Using a tapestry needle, thread the tail through the remaining 6 sts and tie off. Secure all loose ends.

MAKING SNOWMAN'S SCARF

With Color C yarn and circular needle, CO 65 sts.
Row 1: Knit.
Row 2: Purl.
Rows 3–4: Repeat Rows 1–2.
Row 5: Knit.
Loosely BO sts kwise. Break Color C yarn, leaving a 6-inch/ 15-cm tail and tie off. Secure all loose ends.

Felting the Top Hat and Scarf

Once the snowman is felted and stuffed with fiberfill, you can machine felt the hat and scarf until the knit stitches disappear and the pieces are about one third to one half of their original size; this will take one to two cycles. To be sure the hat is the right size, set it on the snowman's head; if it seems too big, continue felting. Once felted, place the hat on the snowman's head and slightly roll up the brim. Press firmly along the brim to flatten it. Indent the crown slightly. When the scarf is the appropriate size, tug it into shape width and lengthwise, then loosely tie it around the snowman's neck and reshape. With a few stickpins, pin the scarf into place to create a windblown look. Allow the hat and scarf to air dry completely in these positions.

Embellishing the Top Hat

Once the hat is dry, cut a length of the black ribbon to fit around the hat as a hatband. Sew or hot glue the ribbon to the hat. Tuck a tiny feather or flower into the band. Perch a miniature red cardinal or a colorful butterfly atop the hat.

To decorate the hat even further, embroider a sprig of holly and a cluster of berries on the felted hat. Using green yarn or embroidery floss and a chenille needle, embroider several straight stitches for the holly sprigs as shown in Diagram 5. Add two or three berries by embroidering

French knots with red yarn or embroidery floss. For embroidery tutorials, see pages 19–24.

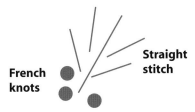

Diagram 5

Adding Fringe to Snowman's Scarf

Once the scarf is dry, cut ten 5-inch/13-cm lengths of Color C yarn. Fold one length in half. Thread the folded end through the eye of a tapestry needle. Direct the needle through the scarf's edge just until the folded end is under the scarf and the tails are above. Remove the needle. Insert the tails through the loop and pull tight, creating a knot at the scarf's edge. Repeat with the remaining pieces of yarn, creating an evenly spaced line of fringe along the edge of each end of the scarf, using five pieces of yarn for each end. With a pair of scissors, trim the fringe to about 1 inch/2.5 cm.

ADDING SNOWMAN'S EYES AND MOUTH

Once the carrot nose is attached, with black yarn and a chenille needle, embroider two French knots for the eyes and one to five knots for the mouth as shown in Diagram 6.

Diagram 6

MAKING SNOWMAN'S CORNCOB PIPE

Poke one end of a toothpick into the side of the cork. To create smoke swirling from the pipe, cut a 4-inch/10-cm length of black 24-gauge wire. Poke the wire into the cork's widest end. Loosely wrap the wire around one of the dpns to create swirls, and one tiny curl at the very end. Poke the toothpick end of the pipe into the mouth area.

Woolly Snowman's arms are completely bendable. Place the fir tree in one of his arms and wrap the arm around the base of the pot, securing it snugly against his body.

MAKING WOOLLY SNOWMAN A POTTED CHRISTMAS TREE

Paint the wooden flowerpot with at least two coats of acrylic paint. Allow it to air dry completely between each coat. With the wire cutters, cut a 3-inch/7.5-cm length from a silk evergreen branch. Trim away a few silk branches nearest the cut end.

　　With a glue gun, squirt hot glue into the flowerpot. Stick the evergreen's cut end into the pot and hold it in an upright position until the glue hardens and cools. For a more tree-like appearance, trim the tree so the branches are wider at the base and tapered at the top.

　　Decorate the tree with a beaded garland. With a 10-inch/25-cm strand of 24-gauge wire, thread and twist the wire around one seed bead. Skip a little space and twist the wire around another bead. Continue until five or six beads are strung along the wire. For the tree's star, twist the wire's end around a large gold bead to secure it in place. To finish, loosely drape the garland around the tree with the large bead resting at the top.

Spooky Stack
of Pumpkins

This felted set of stacked pumpkins is an adaptation of the Woolly Snowman pattern. The pumpkins measure about 8½ inches/21.5 cm tall after being stuffed with fiberfill, not including the topmost stem.

Materials

NOTE: When choosing yarns, do not use a machine washable yarn (like superwash merino) as it will not felt. If making a stack of pumpkins using three different orange colors, be sure to use the same yarn brand throughout to ensure consistent felting. The colors and brands listed are for the pumpkins shown in the photo opposite.

- Color A (bottom pumpkin): 62 yd./57 m 100% wool #4 worsted weight yarn (shown in Cascade 220 Worsted #9444 Tangerine Heather, 220 yd./200 m per skein)
- Color B (middle pumpkin): 29 yd./27 m 100% wool #4 worsted weight yarn (shown using Cascade 220 Worsted #7825 Orange Sherbet, 220 yd./200 m per skein)
- Color C (top pumpkin): 16 yd./15 m 100% wool #4 worsted weight yarn (shown in Cascade 220 Worsted #9465 Burnt Orange, 220 yd./200 m per skein)
- Color D (stem): 1 yd./1 m green 100% wool #4 worsted weight yarn (shown in Cascade 220 Worsted #8914 Granny Smith, 220 yd./200 m per skein)
- US size 10½/6.5 mm set of double-pointed needles
- US size 10½/6.5 mm circular needles, 16 inches/40.5 cm long
- Split-ring stitch marker
- Chenille needle
- Tapestry needle
- Sharp tapestry needle
- Polyester fiberfill stuffing
- Plastic poly-pellets
- Embroidery floss in a coordinating pumpkin color, for furrow lines
- 8-inch/20-cm long upholstery needle
- 1 sheet black acrylic felt, for pumpkin faces
- 38-gauge all-purpose felting needle
- 40-gauge fine felting needle
- Yellow sport weight yarn, for eye highlight dots and decorative optional bow tie
- Sharp scissors
- 1 sheet green wool felt, for leaves
- Green embroidery floss in coordinating color to wool felt, for leaf veins
- Green 24-gauge florist wire, for curly vine
- Wire cutter
- Round-nose pliers

Notes

- If you prefer, all three pumpkins can be knit in the same color orange.
- The pumpkins are knit from the bottom up in the round; the stem is an I-cord knit on the top pumpkin.
- The 40-gauge fine felting needle leaves tinier holes than the larger all-purpose one. It is perfect for working with smaller felt pieces, like the jack-o'-lantern faces.

Spooky Stack of Pumpkins

BOTTOM PUMPKIN

With Color A yarn and dpns, loosely CO 12 sts. Divide the sts evenly among 3 dpns, taking care not to twist them. Join to work in the rnd.

Rnd 1: *Inc 1, k1*; repeat *to* to end of rnd (18 sts). Place a stitch marker to indicate beg of rnd.

Rnd 2: Knit.

Rnd 3: *Inc 1, k2*; repeat *to* to end of rnd (24 sts).

Rnd 4: Knit.

Rnd 5: *Inc 1, k3*; repeat *to* to end of rnd (30 sts).

Rnd 6: Knit.

Rnd 7: *Inc 1, k4*; repeat *to* to end of rnd (36 sts).

Rnd 8: Knit.

Rnd 9: *Inc 1, k5*; repeat *to* to end of rnd (42 sts).

Rnd 10: Change to circular needles, knit.

Rnd 11: *Inc 1, k6*; repeat *to* to end of rnd (48 sts).

Rnd 12: Knit.

Rnd 13: *Inc 1, k7*; repeat *to* to end of rnd (54 sts).

Rnd 14: Knit.

Rnd 15: *Inc 1, k8*; repeat *to* to end of rnd (60 sts).

Rnd 16: Knit.

Rnd 17: *Inc 1, k9*; repeat *to* to end of rnd (66 sts).

Rnds 18–32: Knit.

Rnd 33: *K9, k2tog*; repeat *to* to end of rnd (60 sts).

Rnd 34: Knit.

Rnd 35: *K8, k2togTBL*; repeat *to* to end of rnd (54 sts).

Rnd 36: *K7, k2tog*; repeat *to* to end of rnd (48 sts).

Rnd 37: *K6, k2togTBL*; repeat *to* to end of rnd (42 sts).

Rnd 38: *K5, k2tog*; repeat *to* to end of rnd (36 sts).

Rnd 39: *K4, k2togTBL*; repeat *to* to end of rnd (30 sts).

(continued)

NOTE: If a new color is desired for the middle pumpkin, break Color A yarn, leaving a 6-inch/15-cm tail. If not, continue knitting with the same yarn color.
Rnd 40: Join Color B yarn, knit.

MIDDLE PUMPKIN

Rnd 1: *Inc 1, k4*; repeat *to* to end of rnd (36 sts).
Rnd 2: Knit.
Rnd 3: *Inc 1, k5*; repeat *to* to end of rnd (42 sts).
Rnd 4: Knit.
Rnd 5: *Inc 1, k6*; repeat *to* to end of rnd (48 sts).
Rnd 6: Knit.
Rnd 7: *Inc 1, k7*; repeat *to* to end of rnd (54 sts).
Rnds 8–14: Knit.
Rnd 15: *K7, k2tog*; repeat *to* to end of rnd (48 sts).
Rnd 16: Knit.
Rnd 17: *K6, k2togTBL*; repeat *to* to end of rnd (42 sts).
Rnd 18: *K5, k2tog*; repeat *to* to end of rnd (36 sts).
Rnd 19: *K4, k2togTBL*; repeat *to* to end of rnd (30 sts).
Rnd 20: *K3, k2tog*; repeat *to* to end of rnd (24 sts).
Rnd 21: Knit.
NOTE: If a new color is desired for the top pumpkin, break Color B yarn, leaving a 6-inch/15-cm tail. If not, continue knitting with the same yarn color.

TOP PUMPKIN

Rnd 1: Join Color C yarn, knit.
Rnd 2: *Inc 1, k3*; repeat *to* to end of rnd (30 sts).
Rnd 3: Knit.
Rnd 4: *Inc 1, k4*; repeat *to* to end of rnd (36 sts).
Rnds 5–14: Knit.
Rnd 15: *K4, k2tog*; repeat *to* to end of rnd (30 sts).
Rnd 16: Knit.
Rnd 17: *K3, K2togTBL*; repeat *to* to end of rnd (24 sts).
Rnd 18: *K2, k2tog*; repeat *to* to end of rnd (18 sts).
Rnd 19: *K1, k2togTBL*; repeat *to* to end of rnd (12 sts).
Rnd 20: Knit.
Rnd 21: *K2tog*; repeat *to* to end of rnd (6 sts).
Break Color C yarn, leaving a 6-inch/15-cm tail.

PUMPKIN STEM

Row 1: Join Color D yarn, knit all 6 sts onto one dpn. Do not turn work. Slide the work to the right of the needle.
Rows 2–6: Knit. Do not turn work. Slide the work to the right of the needle.
Break Color D yarn, leaving a 6-inch/15-cm tail. Using a tapestry needle, thread the tail through the remaining 6 sts, from right to left, and tie off. Secure all loose ends. Leave the opening at the pumpkin's base unsewn. Once felted, this opening will allow access to stuff with fiberfill.

Felting and Assembling the Spooky Stack of Pumpkins

Machine felt and stuff the pumpkins as for the Woolly Snowman. Once dry, stuff with fiberfill and poly-pellets as for the snowman and close the bottom opening.

ADDING FURROW LINES

Cut a 2-yd./2-m length of the furrow color embroidery floss. Embroidery floss is sturdier than wool yarn for creating the furrow lines, helping to prevent breakage when pulled firmly. Thread the upholstery needle with the floss, all six plies. Tie a double knot at one end. At the center of the pumpkin's base, sew one or two small stitches to anchor the floss. This knot and stitches will be covered over with a roving blossom end.

Direct the needle up through the pumpkins, coming out where the stem and top pumpkin meet. Direct the needle down to where the top and middle pumpkins meet and into the pumpkin and then up through to the top again, coming out slightly to the left of the first furrow line. Pull the needle until the floss is taut against the pumpkin. The tighter you pull the floss, the deeper the furrow lines. Continue until five furrow lines are evenly spaced around the top pumpkin.

Now direct the needle down and to the base of the top pumpkin again. Direct the needle into where the middle and bottom pumpkins meet and then up through the middle pumpkin, coming out between two of the furrow lines on the top pumpkin. Continue until five furrow lines are evenly spaced around the middle pumpkin. To finish, direct the needle down and into the bottom pumpkin's base, coming out at its center. Sew a small stitch or two at this place to anchor the floss. Bury the end within the pumpkin.

For the base pumpkin, cut and thread the upholstery needle with a 1-yd./1-m length of embroidery floss. Tie a double knot at one end. Sew one or two stitches at the pumpkin's center to anchor. Direct the needle into and up through the bottom pumpkin, coming out between two of the furrow lines on the middle pumpkin. Direct the needle down and into the base, coming out at the same center spot each time. Continue until five furrow lines are evenly spaced around the bottom pumpkin. The base will indent with each pull of the floss. To finish, direct the needle down to the base and sew one or two tiny anchor stitches to secure the floss. Bury the end within the pumpkin. Snip all loose ends.

ADDING THE PUMPKIN BLOSSOM END

Create a blossom end to conceal the knots and any stitching from the furrow lines at the pumpkin's base. Cut several 1-inch/2.5-cm pieces of Color D yarn. Pull the plies apart for each piece and rub them between your fingers to create little balls of yarn fluff. Roll all these pieces together into a loose ball between your palms.

Position the ball of roving over the base, covering the knots and stitching. With the 38-gauge felting needle, poke the roving into a round circle, and then flatten it so it lays firm and smooth against the felted pumpkin. Create and add more yarn roving if needed to completely cover the area. Wet the roving with a little water. Gently rub your wet finger back and forth over the roving to smooth it and eliminate any holes left behind by the felting needle.

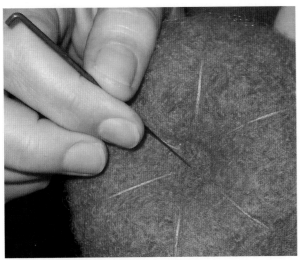

Create a decorative blossom end to conceal the unsightly knots and stitching from the working of the embroidery floss furrow lines.

ADDING THE JACK-O'-LANTERN FACES

The faces shown in Diagram 1 are actual size. Use these templates as a reference or create your own designs. The pieces may need to be trimmed slightly to fit each size pumpkin head.

Use a pair of sharp scissors to cut out the pieces for each pumpkin face from the black acrylic felt. With the

Design Detail: To add a decorative bow, loosely wrap a strand of yellow sport weight yarn around where the top and middle pumpkins meet. Tie a small bow and trim excess lengths.

Actual size

Diagram 1

40-gauge felting needle, begin poking each piece, basting it into position. Stagger the faces slightly from pumpkin to pumpkin so they don't all end up one on top of the other.

Once each piece is basted into position, poke them again to permanently adhere them, until they lay flush and smooth against the wool's surface underneath. To give the eyes a little extra twinkle, create highlight dots by threading a chenille needle with a strand of yellow sport weight yarn. Embroider a small stitch on each eye.

MAKING LEAVES AND CURLY VINES

Cut one small and one large leaf from the piece of green wool felt using the templates in Diagram 2. Wool felt is denser than acrylic, so it gives the leaf more body. Wool felt's color tones are warmer, too, perfect for the leaves. The leaves will be attached to the pumpkins with the wire from the curly vines.

To attach the smaller leaf, thread the sharp-end tapestry needle with a 10-inch/25-cm length of green florist's wire. Direct the needle through the base of the small leaf (1/4 inch/.5 cm from the edge), into the stem's base and out the other side. This secures the leaf to the pumpkin without sewing.

Remove the needle. Cut off the bent end. Adjust the wire so more rests on one side of the stem than the other. To prevent poking wires, create a tiny loop at each wire's end. Wrap each wire around one of the dpns to form curled vines. Create three or four curls on the longer end and two or three curls on the shorter end. Place one curl close to the leaf to hold it firmly in place.

To attach the larger leaf, thread the tapestry needle with another 10-inch/25-cm length of florist's wire. On the pumpkins' right side where the bottom and middle

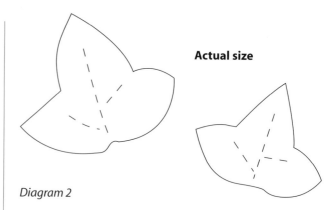

Actual size

Diagram 2

pumpkins meet, direct the needle into the wool and come out again about 1/4 inch/.5 cm away. Remove the needle. Poke both wire ends through the leaf about 1/4 inch/.5 cm apart from each other. Slide the leaf against the pumpkin. Adjust the wires so the longest end is in the back. To prevent poking wires, create a tiny loop at each wire's end. Create curled vines just as you did with the other length of wire, with three or four curls on the back wire and two or three curls on the front. Place one curl close to the leaf to hold it firmly in place.

Before attaching the leaves to your pumpkin stack, add further detail to each leaf by embroidering simple vein lines. Use a chenille needle and a length of green embroidery floss, split into three plies, and embroider either the feather or the straight stitch across the center of each leaf; bury the ends on the back side of each leaf.

Santa Snowman

This jolly old St. Nicholas is a must for every snowman lover's collection! Start with a felted and stuffed Woolly Snowman and then have fun adding all sorts of holiday details, including a padded bag overflowing with tiny toys!

Materials

- 1 felted and stuffed Woolly Snowman, complete with buttons and arms in place, but no facial features
- Red 100% wool roving, for nose
- 38-gauge all-purpose felting needle
- Foam pad
- 1 sheet white acrylic felt, for beard
- Cream-white 100% wool roving, for beard, stocking cap, and mitten trim
- Length of cream worsted weight yarn, for tying beard onto face
- 1 sharp-ended toothpick, for corncob pipe
- $^1/_2$ x $^3/_4$-inch/1.25 x 2-cm cork stopper, for corncob pipe
- 4-inch/10-cm length black 24-gauge wire, for smoke curls (optional)
- 12-inch/31-cm length $^1/_2$-inch-/1.25-cm-wide black pleather, for belt
- 1-inch/2.5-cm square buckle-like button, for belt (LaMode brand buttons, style #24763, has a belt buckle style button)
- Strand of black worsted weight yarn, for eyes
- Color A (stocking cap and mittens): 27 yd./25 m red 100% wool #4 worsted weight yarn
- Color B (toy bag): 37 yd./34 m green 100% wool #4 worsted weight yarn
- US size 10$^1/_2$/6.5 mm set of double-pointed needles
- Split-ring stitch marker
- Tapestry needle
- Chenille needle
- Shoestring, for felting toy bag
- 12-inch/31-cm length red twisted decorative cording, for toy bag
- Dritz® Fray Check liquid sealant, for sealing cord's ends from unraveling
- Miniature toys, for filling toy bag and display purposes
- 1-inch/2.5-cm wooden boxes, for gift boxes
- Holiday wrapping paper, for gift boxes

Notes

- Pleather is a novelty trim sold in fabric stores; it has the look and feel of leather, but it's plastic.
- If a buckle-like button can't be found, replace with a gold or silver square button sewn over the pleather's overlapping ends.

Assembling Santa Snowman

ADDING SANTA'S RED CHERRY NOSE AND COAL-LIKE EYES

Pull off a tiny piece of red roving. Roll it between your fingers to create a nose-size ball. Center the nose on the snowman's face just up from the buttons. With the felting needle, poke the nose's outer edges to the head, securing it so it doesn't pull off when slightly tugged. Round the edges, keeping the nose slightly raised.

With a strand of black worsted yarn and a chenille needle, embroider two French knots for Santa's eyes on either side of his nose (see page 21 for a tutorial). No need to embroider a mouth because his beard will cover that area.

MAKING SANTA'S WHITE BEARD

Using the template in Diagram 1, cut a beard from the sheet of white acrylic felt. The felt will create a firm backing for the roving to be attached to. Place the felt beard on top of the foam pad.

Pull off a small piece of white roving and lay it over the felt beard. Using a felting needle, begin basting the roving onto the felt. Continue to baste on more roving until the felt beard is covered and full looking, occasionally lifting the beard off the foam pad to keep it from adhering.

Once you have the roving basted in place, start to shape and style it. Remember that you want to keep the beard fluffy, so be careful not to overwork it with the felting needle; the more the roving is poked, the denser it will become. Start by rounding out the edges of the

On preceding page: The Santa and his stocking cap and mittens were all knit using Patons Classic Wool Worsted weight yarns: #202 Aran and #230 Bright Red. His toy bag used Cascade 220 Worsted #8267 Forest Green.

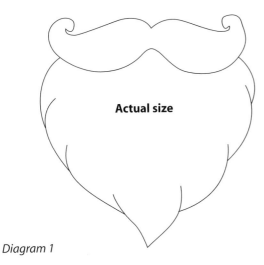

Actual size

Diagram 1

beard with the needle. You can create a slight point or curl at the beard's end by gently pulling and twisting the roving as you pull it with your fingers. By selectively poking the roving with the needle, you can make indents that will give the illusion of tufts and curls, adding more roving if needed.

To give Santa a mustache, place more roving over the top of the beard. Reference the template in Diagram 1 for exact placement. Gently poke all along the mustache edges to adhere it to the beard. Keep the mustache raised and full. Needle felt a small curl at each end of the mustache, if desired.

To finish, use a chenille needle and a 10-inch/25-cm length of white yarn; tie a knot at one end. Insert the needle into one side of the beard, burying the knot on the beard's backside. Attach another length to the other side. Loosely tie the beard onto the Santa's face so the mustache fits snug under the cherry nose. Trim excess lengths.

SANTA'S CORNCOB PIPE

For Santa's pipe, poke an end of the toothpick into the side of the cork. To create smoke swirling from the pipe, poke the length of black wire into the cork's widest end. Loosely wrap the wire around one of the dpns to create swirls, and one tiny curl at the very end. Insert the toothpick end of the pipe through Santa's beard and into the general mouth area.

SANTA'S LEATHER BELT WITH BUCKLE

Wrap the length of pleather around Santa's middle, between the bottom and middle snowballs. Insert one end through the buckle-like button. Trim the end so it tucks behind the buckle's front. Weave the other end through the opposite side of the buckle, and over the first

end. Adjust the belt to fit Santa's middle. Trim any excess, so both ends are concealed behind the buckle.

SANTA'S RED MITTENS WITH FLUFFY WHITE TRIM

Mitten Body

With Color A yarn and dpns, CO 8 sts.
Row 1 (RS): Purl.
Row 2 (WS): Knit.
Row 3: *K1, inc 1*; repeat *to* to end (12 sts).
Row 4: K4, p3, k5. These purl sts will be picked up later for the thumb.
Row 5: Purl.
Row 6: Knit.
Row 7: Purl.
Row 8: *K1, k2tog*; repeat *to* to end (8 sts).
Row 9: *P2tog*; repeat *to* to end (4 sts).
Break Color A yarn, leaving a 10-inch/25-cm tail. With the tapestry needle, thread the tail through the remaining 4 sts and tie off. Fold the mitten in half, RS facing, and with the tapestry needle, loosely sew up the side seam.

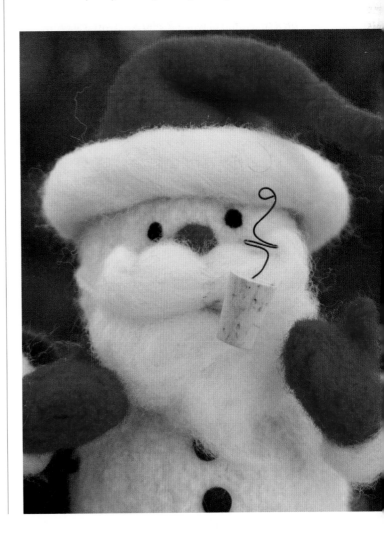

Mitten Thumb

With a dpn, pick up the top loop of each purl stitch mid-way up the mitten. Pick up a total of 3 sts.

Row 1: Join Color A yarn, and knit. Do not turn work. Slide the work to the right of the needle.

Row 2: Knit. Do not turn work. Slide the work to the right of the needle.

Row 3: Knit.

Break Color A yarn, leaving a 6-inch/15-cm tail. With the tapestry needle, thread the tail through the remaining 3 sts from right to left and tie off. Secure the loose ends. Repeat instructions to create a second mitten.

Hand felt both mittens as instructed on page 7 until the knit stitches disappear and the mittens, laid out flat, measure about $1\frac{1}{2}$ inches/4 cm from top to bottom. Watch the felting process of the mittens to ensure that the opening at the bottom of each mitten does not felt shut. Once felted, poke the end of a dpn into the mitten's end to pry it open. Place each felted mitten onto the eraser end of a pencil. Shape each mitten by rounding out the edges and tapering it at the cuff area, so it fits snugly around the pencil. Allow the mittens to air dry completely on the pencils.

Once the mittens are dry, take them off the pencils. Pull off a small strip of white roving and twist it slightly. Position it onto one of the mittens so the two ends meet at the mitten's back. On top of a foam pad, baste the roving along the edge of the mitten with a felting needle. Secure the roving to the mitten so that when tugged, it doesn't pull off. Poke the roving, rounding the trim slightly. As you needle felt the roving, open up the mitten occasionally to prevent it from being needle felted shut. Add more roving if needed to create a fluffy white cuff.

To place the mittens onto the Santa's twig-like hands, bend the first and third fingers backwards and leave the middle finger pointing forward like an arrow. Gently ease on each mitten.

SANTA'S RED STOCKING CAP WITH FLUFFY WHITE TRIM AND POM-POM

With Color A yarn and dpns, CO 30 sts. Divide sts evenly among 3 dpns, taking care not to twist them. Join to work in the rnd.

Rnd 1: Purl. Place a stitch marker to indicate beg of rnd.

Rnds 2–3: Purl.

Rnds 4–8: Knit.

Rnd 9: *K4, k2tog*; repeat *to* to end of rnd (25 sts).

Rnds 10–12: Knit.

Rnd 13: *K3, ssk*; repeat *to* to end of rnd (20 sts).

Rnds 14–16: Knit.

Rnd 17: *K2, k2tog*; repeat *to* to end of rnd (15 sts).

Rnds 18–20: Knit.

Rnd 21: *K1, ssk*; repeat *to* to end of rnd (10 sts).

Rnds 22–24: Knit.

Rnd 25: *K2tog*; repeat *to* to end of rnd (5 sts).

Rnd 26: Knit all sts onto one dpn. Do not turn work. Slide the work to the right of the needle.

Rnds 27–28: Knit. Do not turn work. Slide the work to the right of the needle.

Rnd 29: [K2tog] 2 times, k1 (3 sts). Do not turn work. Slide the work to the right of the needle.

Rnds 30–34: Knit. Do not turn work. Slide the work to the right of the needle.

Break Color A yarn, leaving a 6-inch/15-cm tail. Using a tapestry needle, thread tail through the remaining 3 sts right to left and tie off. Secure all loose ends.

Machine felt the stocking cap as instructed on pages 4–7 until the knit stitches disappear and the cap is about one third to one half its original size. To determine if the cap is done felting, try it on your Santa. If it seems too big, continue felting. Once felted, place the wet hat on Santa's head and shape it to fit, using stickpins to pin it into further shape. Allow the cap to air dry completely in this position.

Once the hat is dry, roll a small pinch of white roving into a ball and place it onto a foam pad. Needle felt the roving into a firm round ball, rotating it so it doesn't flatten or adhere to the pad. Sew the pom-pom to the tip of the stocking cap with a strand of Color A yarn and a chenille needle. Bury the end within the cap. With the tip of the chenille needle, gently fluff up the ball to create a wispy looking pom-pom.

Place the stocking cap back onto the Santa's head. Pull off a strip of white roving about 10 inches/25 cm long and about $1\frac{1}{2}$ inches/4 cm wide. Twist it slightly to create a thick looking cord. Wrap it around the bottom of the cap, overlapping the two ends at the back of the cap. With a felting needle, baste the trim to the cap while it is still on the Santa's head. Secure the roving just enough so it doesn't tug off; you want it to remain as fluffy and wispy looking as possible. The more the trim is poked with the needle, the more it will adhere not only to the cap but to the Santa's head, so as you're doing this, lift up the cap occasionally.

SANTA'S BAG OF TOYS

With Color B yarn and dpns, CO 30 sts. Divide sts evenly among 3 dpns, taking care not to twist them. Join to work in the rnd.

Rnd 1: Purl. Place a stitch marker to indicate beg of rnd.

Rnds 2–4: Knit.

Rnd 5: K3, [yo, k2tog, yo, k2tog, k3] 3 times, yo, k2tog, yo, k2tog, k2 (30 sts).

Rnds 6–7: Knit.

Rnd 8: *Inc 1, k4*; repeat *to* to end of rnd (36 sts).

Rnds 9–23: Knit.

Rnd 24: *K4, k2tog*; repeat *to* to end of rnd (30 sts).

Rnd 25: Knit.

Rnd 26: *K3, ssk*; repeat *to* to end of rnd (24 sts).

Rnd 27: Knit.

Rnd 28: *K2, k2tog*; repeat *to* to end of rnd (18 sts).

Rnd 29: Purl.

Rnd 30: *P1, p2tog*; repeat *to* to end of rnd (12 sts).

Rnd 31: *P2tog*; repeat *to* to end of rnd (6 sts).

Break Color B yarn, leaving a 6-inch/15-cm tail. Using a tapestry needle, thread tail through the remaining 6 sts and tie off. Secure all loose ends. Lace a shoestring through all the holes and tie a loose knot to secure. The shoestring will prevent the holes from closing shut during felting.

Machine felt the toy bag as instructed on pages 4–7. Felt the bag until the individual stitches disappear and the bag is about one third to one half its original size. Once felted, firmly stuff the wet bag with fiberfill until round and full looking, indenting the bottom slightly so it sits upright on the table. Pull out the shoestring. Allow the bag to air dry completely in this position.

Once dry, pull out two thirds of the fiberfill. Leave a third at the bottom of the bag for the toys to rest on. Start at any pair of holes and weave the red cord into the first hole and immediately out the second. Weave in this way through all the holes. Adjust the cord so the ends are equal in length. Trim any excess. Place a small amount of Fray Check® on each end of the cord to keep them from unraveling.

Tuck the miniature toys or packages into the bag, and gently pull the cord snug around them. Dollhouse items make great additions to Santa's bag of toys.

Ho-Ho-Ho! Woolly Santa has come to town!

Tuck a tiny plush bear, candy cane, and a little fir tree into the opening of Santa's toy bag. Miniature dollhouse items make great additions to give the toy bag an overflowing look of whimsical gifts.

Piping Hot Tea Cozy

Keep your pot of tea toasty warm for over an hour under your very own felted wool cozy, personally embellished to fit any occasion!

Felted Measurements

About 13 inches/33 cm wide by 10 inches/25 cm high when laid out flat.

Materials

NOTE: When choosing yarns, do not use a machine washable yarn (like superwash merino) as it will not felt. Also, white yarns generally don't felt well. For a list of cream and other off-white yarns that do felt reliably, see page 2. The yarn color and brand listed are for the tea cozy shown in the photo opposite.

- 313 yd./287 m 100% wool #4 worsted weight yarn in any color (shown in Patons Classic Wool Worsted #84013 Chestnut Tweed, 210 yd./192 m per skein)
- US size 10¹/₂/6.5 mm set of double-pointed needles
- US size 10¹/₂/6.5 mm circular needles, 16 inches/41 cm long
- Stitch marker
- Tapestry needle
- Freezer paper, for appliqué
- Wool felt in your choice of colors, for floral and leaf vine appliqué
- 40-gauge fine felting needle
- Foam pad
- Size 8 or 12 pearl cotton, in colors coordinating with the wool felt
- Size 24-gauge chenille needle
- Sharp scissors
- Seed beads in coordinating colors, any size
- Size 11 beading needle
- FireLine Size B crystal clear braided bead thread

Notes

- Avoid yarns containing mohair for this project. The felted cozy may shed onto your hot teapot.
- The cozy starts with an I-cord that will felt into a convenient little handle to pull the cozy off your pot of tea. The cozy is then knit from the top down in the round. A double-stranded I-cord is then knit around the bottom opening, which will felt into a decorative trim giving the cozy edge added weight.
- For tutorials on blanket stitch and stem stitch, see pages 20 and 24.

Special Stitches

inc 1: Increase one stitch by knitting into the front and then into the back of the same stitch.

ssk: Slip, slip, knit. Slip one stitch as if to knit onto the right needle, then slip another in the same way. Insert the left needle into the front of the two slipped stitches. Knit these stitches together; this creates a left-slanting decrease.

Piping Hot Tea Cozy

TEA COZY KNOT

With two dpns, CO 6 sts. Do not turn work. Slide the work to the right of the needle.

Row 1: Knit. Do not turn work. Slide the work to the right of the needle.

Rep Row 1 until the I-cord is 6 inches/15 cm long. Do not turn work. Slide the work to the right of the needle.

TEA COZY CROWN

Rnd 1: *Inc 1*, repeat *to* to end (12 sts). Divide sts evenly among 3 dpns, taking care not to twist them. Join to work in the rnd.

Rnd 2: *Inc 1*, repeat *to* to end of rnd (24 sts). Place a stitch marker to indicate beg of rnd.

Rnd 3: *Inc 1*; repeat *to* to end of rnd (48 sts).

Rnd 4: Knit.

Rnd 5: *K2, inc 1, k18, inc 1, k2*; repeat *to* to end of rnd (52 sts).

Rnd 6: *K2, inc 1, k20, inc 1, k2*; repeat *to* to end of rnd (56 sts).

Rnd 7: *K2, inc 1, k22, inc 1, k2*; repeat *to* to end of rnd (60 sts).

Rnd 8: *K2, inc 1, k24, inc 1, k2*; repeat *to* to end of rnd (64 sts).

Rnd 9: *K2, inc 1, k26, inc 1, k2*; repeat *to* to end of rnd (68 sts).

Rnd 10: Change to circular needles, knit.

Rnd 11: *K2, inc 1, k28, inc 1, k2*; repeat *to* to end of rnd (72 sts).

Rnd 12: Knit.

(continued)

Rnd 13: *K2, inc 1, k30, inc 1, k2*; repeat *to* to end of rnd (76 sts).

Rnd 14: Knit.

Rnd 15: *K2, inc 1, k32, inc 1, k2*; repeat *to* to end of rnd (80 sts).

Rnd 16: Knit.

Rnd 17: *K2, inc 1, k34, inc 1, k2*; repeat *to* to end of rnd (84 sts).

Rnd 18: Knit.

Rnd 19: *K2, inc 1, k36, inc 1, k2*; repeat *to* to end of rnd (88 sts).

Rnd 20: Knit.

Rnd 21: *K2, inc 1, k38, inc 1, k2*; repeat *to* to end of rnd (92 sts).

Rnd 22: Knit.

Rnd 23: *K2, inc 1, k40, inc 1, k2*; repeat *to* to end of rnd (96 sts).

Rnd 24: Knit.

Rnd 25: *K2, inc 1, k42, inc 1, k2*; repeat *to* to end of rnd (100 sts).

Rnds 26–85: Knit 60 rounds.

Rnd 86: Knit 25 sts, break yarn, leaving a 6-inch/15-cm tail.

TEA COZY BOTTOM CORDING

With two dpns and two strands of yarn, CO 3 sts. The double stranding appears as two stitches on the needle but knit them as one. Begin knitting the I-cord bind-off as follows: Slide the 3 sts from the dpn onto tip of left circular needle. With the dpn, knit first 2 sts off. Slip next stitch as if to knit. Knit another stitch from circular needle. Pass slipped stitch over previously knitted stitch and off the needle. Slide the 3 sts from the dpn back onto the circular needle. Repeat this process until you have bound off all the sts on the circular needle and there are 3 sts on the dpn.

Break yarn, leaving a 6-inch/15-cm tail. Using a tapestry needle, thread tail through the remaining 3 sts from right to left and tie off. Sew both ends to the cozy and to one another, overlapping them slightly to appear as one continuous cord. Secure all loose ends.

Felting the Tea Cozy

Machine felt the cozy as directed on pages 4–7 until the knit stitches disappear and the wet cozy laid out flat measures about 13 inches/33 cm wide by 10 inches/25 cm high. It will take one to two cycles to felt the cozy. Be sure to check on the cozy periodically as it is felting.

Once felted, tug and pull the wet cozy into the desired shape. Tie the cozy's top cord into a loose knot. Stuff the cozy with paper towels or plastic bags to fill out its shape and stand upright on a wire rack. Allow the tea cozy to air dry completely in this position.

How to Brew a Proper Cup of Tea

Here is my method for brewing the perfect pot of tea, using loose tea leaves or tea bags (Darjeeling and Ceylon tea are my personal favorites).

1. Boil a kettle of freshly drawn cold water. Pour about 1 inch/2.5 cm of hot water into a six-cup teapot. Swirl the water to warm the pot. Pour the water out and measure 1 teaspoon/5 mL of loose-leaf tea for each cup and one for the pot (about 7 teaspoons/35 ml) into the pot. (If you prefer tea bags, use one tea bag per cup and one for the pot.)

2. Add rapidly boiling water to the teapot and stir once. Place the lid on the teapot and cover with the tea cozy to keep the tea warm while brewing. Set the timer for four to five minutes.

3. When the tea is brewed, stir once. Using a tea strainer, strain the tea into each cup.

If the tea leaves/bags are not removed from the pot, your tea will continue to brew, which means that the tea at the bottom of the pot will be stronger and possibly even bitter. To prevent this, strain the brewed tea immediately into a second warmed pot.

Now, gather together a rustic basket, your newly felted tea cozy, a box of loose-leaf Darjeeling tea, and a batch of freshly baked classic cream scones, and you have a delightful gift for your favorite tea-drinker!

Embellishing the Tea Cozy

The felted tea cozy lends itself to hours of playful embellishing, presenting a blank canvas to create a work of art. The flower and vine appliqué shown in the photo on page 118 is made using wool appliqué, simple embroidery, and a few colorful seed beads.

For the appliqué design as shown, you'll need to cut from the felt the shapes using the templates provided in Diagram 1 on page 122:

- 1 large flower (harvest gold)
- 1 large flower center (burnt red)
- 9 small round flowers (yellow-gold)
- 6 small round flower centers (burnt red)
- 13 leaves (mossy green)

For the vines, cut three ¼ x 10-inch/.5 x 25-cm lengths out of green wool felt. Trace the other templates onto the paper (not shiny) side of a sheet of freezer paper. Cut them out, and then lightly adhere the paper templates to the wool felt by pressing on them with a hot, dry iron, so the paper sticks to the felt. With a pair of scissors, cut along the paper edges through the felt, and then peel away the paper. With a felting needle, lightly poke the pieces into place on the cozy according to the template in Diagram 1 or the way you want them. Straight pins can be used instead of needle felting to hold the pieces in place. You want the vines to curve slightly, so ease them along as you needle felt them into position. Tuck the vine ends under the flowers.

Once the pieces are in position, embroider the stem stitch down the center of each vine. This will hold the felt vines in place.

Next, embroider the blanket stitch along the outside edge of the largest flower, adhering it to the cozy. Also use the blanket stitch to attach the flower's center on top of this base flower.

Sew the circle flowers into position using a series of straight stitches. Starting at the center of the flower, direct the needle out to the circle's edge, down, and then back up into the center as shown in the photo below

right, and continue until six even lines are embroidered. Repeat this for all the felt circles.

Next, embroider each leaf into position using the overhand stitch. For placement, refer to Diagram 1. Once each leaf is in position, embroider decorative vein lines down the leaf's center using the feather stitch and the same embroidery floss color used to sew on the leaves.

Once all the felt pieces are embroidered, the beads can be added to the design.

Thread a bead needle with a strand of clear thread and follow the directions on page 26 for sewing on beads. Sew burnt-red beads along the vine as shown in Diagram 1 and sew beads on the center of the main flower: two green and three burnt-red beads.

On the cozy's front side only, sew a green bead into each flower's center on three of the round flowers (flowers without the red felt center). For the other six circle flowers, sew both the small red felt circle and a green bead to the gold flower's center. Come up from the bottom of your work, and direct the beading needle up through the red circle. Slip a bead onto the needle. Direct the needle back through the red felt, bypassing the bead, and into the flower and cozy wool underneath. Pull the floss so the felt and bead rest taut against the flower underneath. Repeat this for all six flowers.

The embroidered lines radiate out from the felt's center, adding more color as well as holding the circle in place.

Pieces of wool felt along with coordinated colored seed beads and embroidery floss are all the materials needed to transform a solid color tea cozy into a functional work of art!

This close-up photo shows the detailing of the appliqué design: the stem stitch embroidered along the green veins, the feather stitch on top of each leaf, and the addition of seed beads for little bursts of color throughout the design.

Diagram 1

Actual size

Tea Cozy's front side

Tea Cozy's back side